THE

HISTORY OF EDUCATION IN VIRGINIA

DURING

THE SEVENTEENTH CENTURY.

PREPARED FOR

U. S. COMMISSIONER OF EDUCATION,

BY

EDWARD D. NEILL.

WASHINGTON:
GOVERNMENT PRINTING OFFICE.
1867.

I. VIRGINIA.

PERIOD I. 1618–1700.

VIRGINIA COMPANY.

The Virginia Company were the first to take steps relative to the establishment of schools in the English colonies of America. In a letter written to the authorities of the infant settlement at Jamestown, on November 18, 1618, they use these words: "Whereas, by a special grant and license from his Majesty, a general contribution over this realm hath been made for the building and planting of a college for the training up of the children of those infidels in true religion, moral virtue, and civility, and for other godliness, we do therefore, according to a former grant and order, hereby ratify and confirm and ordain that a convenient place be chosen and set out for the planting of a university at the said Henrico in time to come, and that in the mean time preparation be there made for the building of the said college for the children of the infidels, according to such instructions as we shall deliver. And we will and ordain that ten thousand acres, partly of the land they impaled, and partly of the land within the territory of the said Henrico, be allotted and set out for the endowing of the said university and college with convenient possessions."

A week after the date of this communication, a ripe scholar in England, the Rev. Thomas Lorkin, subsequently distinguished as secretary of the English embassy in France, writes to an acquaintance: "A good friend of mine proposed to me within three or four days a condition of going over to Virginia, where the Virginia Company means to erect a college, and undertakes to procure me good assurance of £200 a year, and if, I shall find there any ground of dislike, liberty to return at pleasure."

The offer, after due consideration, appears not to have been accepted, and nothing more was done until the reorganization of the company in April, 1619, and the election of Sir Edwin Sandys as its presiding officer.

By his integrity, patriotism, scholarship, and great administrative talent, he infused new life into the expiring society, and associated with him Nicholas Ferrar, the honorable merchant of London, Sir John Danvers, the step-father, and Edward Lord Cherbury, the brother of the sweet poet, George Herbert, also the Earl of Southampton, who in early life extended a helping hand to a poor boy that is said to have held horses for gentlemen at the doors of play-houses, and became Shakspeare, the portrayer of all the varied emotions of the soul, whose reputation as a dramatist has increased in lustre as the centuries have advanced.

The new managers of the company proceeded to reconstruct Virginia with the most liberal views. By their permission the first representative and legislative body in America was convened at Jamestown, on July 30, 1619, in the church, the most convenient place they could find, the minister of which was Mr. Buck.

During the sessions of this body, which continued until the fourth of August, a petition was presented relative to the erection of a university and college. From this period until the dissolution of the Virginia Company the design of a university and college was never forgotten.

The collections taken up by order of the King for a college in 1619 amounted to £2,043 2*s.* 12½*d.*, and at a meeting of the company on May 26th, Sir Edwin Sandys, as treasurer, propounded to the court "a thing worthy to be taken into consideration for the glory of God and honor of the company, forasmuch as the King, in his most gracious favour, hath granted his letters to the several bishops of his kingdom for the collecting of moneys to erect and build a college in Virginia for the training and bringing up of infidels' children to the true knowledge of God and understanding of righteousness. He conceived it the fittest that as yet they should not build the college, but rather forbear awhile, and begin first with the advances they have to provide and settle an annual revenue, and out of that to begin the erection of said college. And for the performance hereof also moved that a certain piece of land be laid out at Henrico, being the place formerly resolved on, which should be called the college land, and for the planting of the same send presently fifty good persons, to be located thereon, and to occupy the same."

On June 14, 1619, it was moved by Mr. Treasurer, "that the court would take into consideration to appoint a committee of their gentlemen and other of his Majesty's counsel for Virginia concerning the college, being a weighty business, and so great that an account of their proceedings therein must be given to the State. Upon which the court, upon deliberate consideration, have recommended the rare trust unto the right worthy Sir Dudley Diggs, Sir John Danvers, Sir Nath. Rich, Sir Jo. Wolstenholme, Mr. Deputy Ferrar, Mr. Dr. Anthony, and Mr. Dr. Gulson, to meet at such time as Mr. Treasurer shall order thereto."

On June the 24th the committee by the last court appointed for the college having met, as they were desired, delivered over their proceedings, which the court allowed, being this that followeth:

"A note of what kind of men and most fit to be sent to Virginia in the next intended voyage of transporting one hundred men.

"A minister to be entertained at the yearly allowance of forty pounds, and to have fifty acres of land for him and his forever; to be allowed his transportation and his man's at the company's charge, and ten pounds to furnish himself withall.

"A captain thought fit, to be considered of, to take charge of such *people as are to be planted on the college land.*

"All the people at this first sending, except some soon to be sent as well for planting the college and public land, to be single men, unmarried.

"A warrant to be made and directed to Sir Thomas Smith for the payment of the collection money to Sir Edwin Sandys, treasurer, and that Dr. Gulstone shall be entreated to present unto my Lord Primate of Canterbury such letters to be signed for the speedy paying of the moneys from every diocese which yet remain unpaid.

"The several sorts of tradesmen and others for the college land: smiths, carpenters, bricklayers, turners, potters, husbandmen, brickmakers.

"And whereas, according to the standing order, seven were chosen by the court to be of the committee for the college, the said order allowing no more, and, inasmuch as Mr. John Wroth came in error to be left out, he is therefore now desired to be an assistant with them, and to give them meeting at such time and place as is agreed of."

At a meeting of the company held in London, at Mr. Ferrar's house, on July 21, 1619, the Earls of Southampton and Warwick, Sir Thomas Gates, and others being present, the following anonymous letter was read:

+
I. H. S.

"SIR EDWIN SANDYS, *Treasurer of Virginia:*

"Good luck in the name of the Lord, who is daily magnified by the experiment of your zeal and piety in giving beginning to the foundation of the college in Virginia, sacred work due to Heaven and so longed for on earth.

"Now know we assuredly that the Lord will do you good and bless you in all your proceedings, even as He blessed the house of Obed Edom and all that pertaineth unto him because of the ark of God. Now that you seek the kingdom of God, all things shall be ministered unto you. This I well see already, and perceive that by your godly determination the Lord hath given you favor in the sight of all His people, and I know some whose hearts are much enlarged because of the house of the Lord our God to procure you wealth, which greater designs I have presumed to outrun with this oblation, which I humbly beseech you may be accepted as the pledge of my devotion, and as an earnest of the power which I have vowed unto the Almighty God of Jacob concerning this thing, which till I may in part perform I desire to remain unknown and unsought after.

"The things are these: a communion cup with the ewer and vase; a trencher plate for the bread; a carpet of crimson velvet; a linen damask cloth."

On Wednesday, November 17, 1619, at a great and general quarterly meeting of the Virginia Company, the treasurer referred to the instructions sent out by the new governor of the colony, Sir George Yeardley, by which were to be selected ten thousand acres of land for the university to be planted at Henrico, of which one thousand was reserved for the college for the conversion of infidels.

On December 1st, "It was propounded that in consideration of some public gifts given by sundry persons to Virginia, divers presents of church plate and other ornaments, two hundred pounds already given toward building a church, and five hundred pounds promised by another toward the educating of infidels' children, that, for the honor of God, and memorial of such good benefactors, a tablet might hang in the court with their names and gifts inserted, and the ministers of Virginia and the Sommer islands may have intelligence thereof, that for their pious works they may recommend them to God in their prayers; which generally was thought very fit and expedient."

On February 2, 1619–20: "A letter from an unknown person was read, directed to the treasurer, promising five hundred pounds for the educating and bringing up infidels' children in Christianity, which Mr. Treasurer, not willing to meddle therewith alone, desired the court to appoint a select committee for the managing and employing of it to the best purpose. They made choice of: Lord Pagett, Sir Tho. Wroth, Mr. J. Wroth, Mr. Deputie, Mr. Tho. Gibbs, Dr. Winstone, Mr. Bamfourde, and Mr. Keightley.

The copy of the letter.

"SIR: Your charitable endeavour for Virginia hath made you a father, me a favourer of those good works which, although heretofore hath come near to give birth, yet for want of strength could never be delivered, (envy and division dashing these younglings even in the womb,) until your helpful hand, with other favorable personages, gave them both birth and being, for the better prosecuting of which good and pious work, seeing many casting gifts into the treasury, I am encouraged to tender my poor mite; and although I cannot with the princes of Issaker bring gold and silver covering, yet offer you what I can, some goats' hair, necessary stuff for the Lord's tabernacle, protesting here in my sincerity, without Papistical merit or Pharisaical applause, wishing from my heart as much unity in your honorable undertaking as there is sincerity in my designs, to the furtherance of which good work, the converting of infidels to the faith of Christ, I promised by my good friends £500 for the maintenance of a convenient number of young Indians taken at the age of seven years, or younger, and instructed in the reading and understanding the principles of Christianity unto the age of twelve years, and then as occasion showeth, to be trained and brought up in some lawful trade with all humanity and gentleness until the age of one and twenty years, and then to enjoy like liberties and privileges with our native English in that place.

"And for the better performance thereof you shall receive £50 more, which shall be delivered into the hands of two religious persons with certitude of payment, who shall unto every quarter examine and certify to the treasurer here, in England, the due operation of these promises, together with the names of those children thus taken, the foster-fathers and overseers, not doubting but you are all assured that gifts devoted to God's service cannot be diverted to private and secular advantages without sacrilege. If your graver judgments can devise a more charitable course for the younger, I beseech you inform my friend, with your security for true performance, and my benevolence shall be always ready to be delivered accordingly.

"The greatest courtesy I expect or crave is to conceal my friend's name, lest importunity might urge him to betray that trust of service, which he hath faithfully promised, who hath moved my heart to this good work. I rest, ab famo,

"DUST AND ASHES.

"Sir Edwin Sandys,

"*The faithful Treasurer for Virginia.*"

On the sixteenth of February the following was passed:

"Whereas, at the last court a special committee was appointed for the managing of the £500 given by an unknown person for educating the infidels' children, Mr. Treasurer signified that they have met and taken into consideration the proposition of Sir John Wolstenholme, that John Peirce and his associates might have the training and bringing up of some of these children; but the said committee, for divers reasons, think it inconvenient, first, because they intend not to go this two or three months, and then after their arrival will be long in settling themselves; as also that the Indians are not acquainted with them, and so they may stay four or five years before they have account that any good is done.

"And for to put it into the hands of private men to bring them up, as was by some proposed, they thought it was not so fit, by reason of the difficulty unto which it is subject.

"But forasmuch as divers hundreds and particular plantations are already there settled, and the Indians well acquainted with them, as namely, Smith's Hundred, Martin's Hundred, Bartlett's Hundred, and the like, that, therefore, they receive and take charge of them, by which course they shall be sure to be well nurtured and have their due so long as these plantations shall hold; and for such of the children as they find capable of learning shall be put in the college and brought up to be Fellows, and such as are not shall be put to trades and be brought up in the fear of God and the Christian religion.

"And being demanded how and by what lawful means they would preserve them, and after keep them, that they run not to join their parents or friends, and their parents or friends steal them not away, which natural affection may inforce in the one and the other, it was answered and well allowed that a treaty and agreement be made with the King of that country concerning them, which if it so fall out at any time, as is expressed, they may by his command be returned.

"Whereupon Sir Thomas Roe promised that Bartlett's Hundred should take two or three, and Mr. Smith to be respondent to the company, and because every hundred may the better consider thereof they were licensed till Sunday in the afternoon, at which time they sit at Mr. Treasurer's to bring in their answer how many they will have, and bring those that will be respondent for them, and those that others will not take Mr. Treasurer, in behalf of Smith's Hundred, hath promised to take into their charge."

"The Treasurer signified, on February 22d, "that the corporation of Smith's Hundred very well accepted of the charge of infidels' childrenre commended unto them by the court, in regard of their good disposition to do good; but, otherwise, if the court shall please to take it from them they will willingly give £100. And for their resolutions, although they have not yet set them down in writing, by reason of some things yet to be considered of, they will, so soon as may be, prepare the same and present it."

A box standing upon the table with this direction, "*To Sir Edwin Sandis, the faithful Treasurer for Virginia*," he acquainted them that it was brought unto him by a man of good fashion, who would neither tell him his name nor from whence it came; but, by the subscription being the same as the letter, he considered that it might be the £550 promised them.

And it being agreed that the box should be opened, there was a bag of new gold containing the said sum of £550.

Whereupon Doctor Winstone reporting that the committee had requested for the managing thereof, and that it should be wholly in charge of Smith's Hundred. It was desired by some that the resolution should be presented in writing at the next court, which, in regard of the Ash-Wednesday sermon, was agreed to be upon Thursday afternoon.

At a meeting held at the house of Sir Edwin Sandys, on April 9, 1620, intelligence was given that Mr. Nicholas Ferrar, elder, being translated from this life unto a better, had by his will bequeathed £300 towards the converting of infidels' children in Virginia, to be paid unto Sir Edwin Sandys and Mr. Jo. Ferrar, at such time as, upon certificate from there, ten of the said infidels' children shall be placed in the college, to be there disposed of by the said Sir Edwin Sandys and Jo. Ferrar, according to the true intent of the said will; and that in the mean [time] till that was performed he hath tied his executors to pay eight per cent. for the same unto three several honest men in Virginia, (such as the said Sir Edwin Sandys and John Ferrar shall approve of,) of good life and fame, that will undertake each of them to bring up one of the said children in the grounds of Christian religion, that is to say, £8 yearly apiece.

About this period Mr. George Thorpe, a gentleman of sterling character, of his Majesty's privy chamber, and one of his council for Virginia, sailed for the colony, having been appointed by the company deputy to take charge of the college lands.

At a meeting of the company on November 15, 1620, as the reading of the minutes of the previous meeting were completed, "a stranger stepped in," and presented a map of Sir Walter Raleigh's, containing a description of Guiana, and with the same four great books, as the gift of one that desired his name might not be known. One of these was a translation of St. Augustine's City of God; the others were the works of the distinguished Calvinist and Puritan, Mr. Perkins, "which books the donor desired might be sent to the college in Virginia, there to remain in safety to the use of the collegiate educators, and not suffered at any time to be lent abroad."

For which so worthy a gift my lord of Southampton desired the party that presented them to return deserved thanks from himself and the rest of the company to him that had so kindly bestowed them.

The next year the interest of the company in establishing schools in America was increased by another unexpected donation.

The Rev. Patrick Copeland,* a devout man, like the celebrated and accomplished Henry Martyn, a century and a half later, became a chaplain of the East India Company, and in 1613 arrived at Surat. The next year there was sent to England an East India youth, that had been taught to read and write by Mr. Copeland, and he was sent to school by the East India Company, "to be instructed in religion, that hereafter he may be sent home to convert some of his nation."

On July 18, 1615, letters were read at a meeting of the East India Company from Patrick Copeland, informing them how much the Indian youth recommended to his care had profited in the knowledge of the Christian religion, so that he is able to render an account of his faith and desiring to receive directions concerning his baptism, "being of opinion that it was fit to have it publicly effected, being the first fruits of India." The company instructed their deputy to speak with Abbot, archbishop of Canterbury, to understand his opinion before they resolved on anything in so weighty a matter.

Mr. Copeland returning home from India in 1621, met some ships on the way to Virginia, and learning the destitution of the New World

* The manuscript records spell the name in two ways, Copland and Copeland.

colony in churches and schools, he longed to do them good. The mode devised for helping them is fully explained in the minutes of the Virginia Company.

At a court held 24th October, 1621, Mr. Deputy acquainted the court "that one Mr. Copland, a minister lately returned from the East Indies, out of an earnest desire to give some furtherance unto the plantation in Virginia, had been pleased, as well by his own good example as by persuasion, to stir up many that came with him in the ship called the Royal James to contribute toward some good work to be begun in Virginia, insomuch that he had already procured a matter of some £70 to be employed that way, and had also written from Cape Bona Speranza to divers parties in the East Indies to move them to some charitable contribution thereunto. So, as he hoped, they would see very shortly his letters would produce some good effect among them, especially if they might understand in what manner they intended to employ the same. It was therefore ordered that a committee should be appointed to treat with Mr. Copland about it. And forasmuch as he had so well deserved of the company by his extraordinary care and pains in this business, it was thought fit and ordered that he should be admitted a free brother of this company, and at the next quarter court it should be moved that some proportion of land might be bestowed upon him in gratification of his worthy endeavors to advance this extended work; and further, it was thought fit also to add thereunto a number of some other special benefactors unto the plantation whose memorial is preserved. The committee to treat with him are these: Mr. Deputy, Mr. Gibbs, Mr. Nicholas Ferrar, Mr. Bamforde, Mr. Abra. Chamberlyne, Mr. Roberts, Mr. Ayres."

On the last of October, 1621, Mr. Deputy signified that, "forasmuch as it was reserved unto the company to determine whether the said money should be employed towards the building of a church or a school, as aforesaid, your committee appointed have had conference with Mr. Copland about it, and do hold it fit, for many important reasons, to employ the said contribution towards the erection of a public free school in Virginia, towards which an unknown person hath likewise given £30, as may appear by the report of said committee, now presented to be read.

"At a meeting of the committee on Tuesday, the 30th of October, 1621, present Mr. Deputy, Mr. Gibbs, Mr. Wroth, Mr. Ayres, Mr. Nicholas Ferrar, Mr. Roberts.

"The said committee meeting this afternoon to treat with Mr. Copland touching the dispose of the money given by some of the East India Company that came with him in the Royal James, to be bestowed upon some good work for the benefit of the plantation in Virginia, the said Mr. Copland did deliver in a note the names of those that had freely and willingly contributed their moneys hereunto, which money Mr. Copland said they desired might be employed towards the building either of a church or school in Virginia, which the company should think fit. And that although the sum of money was but a small proportion to perform so great a work, yet Mr. Copland said he doubted not but to persuade the East India Company, whom he meant to solicit, to make some addition thereunto; besides, he said that he had very effectually wrote (the copy of which letter he delivered and was read) to divers factories in the East Indies to stir them up to the like contribution towards the performance of this pious work, as they had already done for a church at Wapping, to which, by his report, they have given about £400.

"It being, therefore, now taken into consideration whether a church or a school was most necessary, and might nearest agree to the intentions of the donors, it was considered that forasmuch as each particular plantation, as well as the general, either had or ought to have a church appropriated unto them, there was therefore a greater want of a school than of churches.

"As also for that it was impossible, with so small a proportion, to compass so great a work as the building of a church would require, they therefore conceived it most fit to resolve for the erecting of a public free school, which, being for the education of children and grounding them in the principles of religion, civility of life, and human learning, seemed to carry with it the greatest weight and highest consequence unto the plantations, as that whereof both church and commmonwealth take their original foundation and happy estate, this being also so like to prove a work most acceptable unto the planters, through want whereof they have been hitherto constrained to send their children from thence hither to be taught.

"Secondly. It was thought fit that the school should be placed in one of the four cities, and they conceived that Charles City, of the four, did afford the most convenient place for that purpose, as well in respect it matcheth with the best in wholesomeness of air, as also for the commodious situation thereof, being not far distant from Henrico and other particular plantations.

"It was also thought fit that, in honor of the East India benefactors, the same should be called the East India School, who shall have precedence before any other to present their children there, to be brought up in the rudiments of learning.

"It was also thought fit that this, as a collegiate or free school, should have dependence upon the college in Virginia, which should be made capable to receive scholars from the school into such scholarships; and fellowships of said college shall be endowed withal for the advancement of scholars as they arise by degrees and desert in learning.

"That, for the better maintenance of the schoolmaster and usher intended there to be placed, it was thought fit that it should be moved at the next quarter court that one thousand acres of land should be allotted unto the said school, and that tenants, besides an overseer of them, should be forthwith sent upon this charge, in the condition of apprentices, to manure and cultivate said land; and that, over and above this allowance of land and tenants to the schoolmaster, such as send their children to the school should give some benevolence unto the schoolmaster, for the better increase of his maintenance.

"That it should be specially recommended to the governor to take care that the planters there be stirred up to put their helping hands towards the speedy building of the said school, in respect that their children are likely to receive the greatest benefit thereby, in their education; and to let them know that those that exceed others in their bounty and assistance hereunto shall be privileged with the preferment of their children to these said schools before others that shall be found less worthy.

"It is likewise thought fit that a good schoolmaster be provided, forthwith to be sent unto this school.

"It was also informed, by a gentleman of this committee, that he knew one, that desired not to be named, that would bestow £30, to be added to the former sum of £70 to make it an £100, towards the building of the said school."

This report, being read, was well approved of, and thought fit to be referred for confirmation to the next quarter court. On November 19, 1621, the company again considered the matter.

"Whereas the committee appointed to treat with Mr. Copland about the building of the East India church, or school, in Virginia, towards which a contribution of £70 was freely given by some of the East India Company that came home in the Royal James, did now make report what special reasons moved them to resolve for the bestowing of that money towards the erection of a school, rather than a church, which report is at large set down at a court held last October.

"And further, that they had allowed one thousand acres of land and five apprentices, besides an overseer, to manure, besides that benevolence that is hoped will be given by each man that sends his children thither to be taught, for the schoolmaster's maintenance in his first beginning; which allowance of land and tenants, being put to the question, was well approved of, and referred for confirmation to the quarter court: provided that in the establishment hereof the company reserve unto themselves power to make laws and orders for the better government of the said school and the revenues and profits that shall thereunto belong.

"It was further moved that, in respect to Mr. Copland, minister, hath been a chief cause of procuring this former contribution to be given by the aforesaid company, and had also writ divers letters to many factories in the East Indies to move them to follow this good example, for the better advancement of this pious work, that therefore the company would please to gratify him with some proportion of land.

"Whereupon the court, taking it into consideration, and being also informed that Mr. Copland was furnishing out persons to be transported this present voyage to plant and inhabit upon said lands as should be granted unto them by the company, they were the rather induced to bestow upon him an extraordinary gratification of three shares of land, old adventure, which is three hundred acres, upon a first division, without paying rent to the company, referring the further ratification of the said gift to the quarter court, as also his admittance of being a free brother of this company."

About this time a young Puritan minister, John Brinsley, a nephew of the English Seneca, the distinguished Bishop Hall, and the private secretary of his uncle at the synod of Dort, who in after life became the author of many classical and theological treatises, prepared a little book suitable for the projected school in Virginia.*

* In 1622 Brinsley published "A Consolation for our Grammar Schooles; or a faithful and most comfortable encouragement for laying of a sure foundation of a good learning in our schooles, and for prosperous building therefor; more specially for all those of the inferior sort, and all rude countries and places, namely, for Ireland, Wales, Virginia, with the Sommer islands, and for their more speedie attaining of our English tongue by the same labour, that all may speake one and the same language. And withall, for the helping of all such as are derirous speedlie to recover that which they had formerlie got in the grammar schooles: and to proceed aright therein, for the perpetual benefit of these our nations, and of the churches of Christ. London: Printed by Richard Field, for Thomas Mann, dwelling in Paternoster Row, at the sign of the Talcot; 1622."

At a court held for Virginia the 19th of December, 1621, Mr. Balmfield signified unto the court of a book "compiled by a painful schoolmaster, one Mr. John Brinsley;" whereupon the court gave order that the company's thanks should be given unto him, and appointed a select committee to peruse the said book, viz: Sir John Danvers, Mr. Deputy, Mr. Gibbs, Mr. Wroth, Mr. Bamfield, Mr. Copland, Mr. Ayres, and Mr. Nicho. Farrar, who are entreated to meet when Mr. Deputy shall appoint, and after to make report of their opinions touching the same at the next court.

At a court held for Virginia, on Wednesday, the 16th January, 1621, [1622,] the committee appointed to peruse the book which Mr. John Brinsley, schoolmaster, presented at the last court, touching the education of the younger sort of scholars, forasmuch as they had as yet no time to peruse the same, by reason of many businesses that did arise, they desired of the court some longer respite, which was granted unto them. Mr. Copland, being present, was entreated to peruse it in the mean time, and deliver his opinion thereof to the committee, at their meeting, about it.

At a quarter court held on January 30, 1621–'2, "the letter subscribed D. and A., brought to the former court by an unknown messenger, was now again presented to be read, the contents whereof are as follows:

"'January 28th, 1621.

"'Most Worthy Company: Whereas I sent the Treasurer and yourselves a letter, subscribed 'Dust and Ashes,' which promised £550, and did, some time afterward, according to my promise, send the said money to Sir Edwin Sandys, to be delivered to the company. In which letter I did not directly order the bestowing of the said money, but showed my interest for the conversion of infidels' children, as it will appear by that letter, which I desire may be read in open court, wherein I chiefly commended the ordering thereof to the wisdom of the honorable company. And whereas the gentlemen of Southampton Hundred have undertaken the disposing of the said £550, I have long attended to see the erecting of some schools, or other way whereby some of the children of the Virginians might have been taught and brought up in the Christian religion and good manners, which are not being done according to my intent, but the money detained by a private hundred all this while, contrary to my mind, though I judge very charitably of that honorable society. And as already you have received a great and the most painfully gained part of my estate towards the laying of the foundation of the Christian religion, and helping forward of this pious work in that heathen, now Christian, land, so now I require of the whole body of the honorable and worthy company, whom I entrusted with the disposal of said moneys, to see the same speedily and faithfully converted to the work intended. And I do further propound to your honorable company, that if you will procure that some of the male children of the Virginians, though but a few, be brought over into England here to be educated and taught, and to wear a habit as the children of Christ's Hospital do, and that you will be pleased to see the £550 converted to this use, then I faithfully promise to add £450 more, to make the sum £1,000, which, if God permit, I will cheerfully send you, only I desire to nominate the first tutor or governor who shall take charge to nurse and instruct them. But if you, in your wisdom, like not this motion, then my humble suit unto the whole body of your honorable company is that my former gift of £550 be wholly employed and bestowed upon a free school to be erected in Southampton Hundred, so it be presently employed, or such other place as I or my friends shall well like, wherein both English and Virginians may be taught together, and that the said school be endowed with such privileges as you, in your wisdom, shall think fit. The master of which school, I humbly crave, may not be allowed to go over except he first bring to the company sound testimony of his sufficiency in learning and sincerity of life.

"'The Lord give you wise and understanding hearts, that his work therein be not negligently performed.

"'D. and A.

"'*The Right Honorable and Worthy the*
"'Treasurer, Council, and Company of Virginia.'"

The letter being referred to the consideration of this court, forasmuch as it did require an account of this company how they have expended the said money, viz: the £550 in gold for the bringing up of the infidels' children in true religion and Christianity, Sir Edwin Sandys declared that the said money coming unto him enclosed in a box in the time of his being treasurer, not long after a letter subscribed "Dust and Ashes" had been directed unto him in the quality of treasurer, and delivered in the court and there openly read. He brought the money also to the next court in the box unopened, whereupon the court, after a large and serious deliberation how the said money might be best employed to the use intended, at length resolved that it was fittest to be entertained by the societies of Southampton Hundred and Martin's

Hundred, and easy to undertake for a certain number of infidels' children to be brought up by them and amongst them in Christian religion, and some good trade to live by according to the donor's religious desire.

But Martin's Hundred desired to be excused by reason their plantation was sorely weakened and then in much confusion; wherefore it being pressed that Southampton Hundred should undertake the whole, they also considering, together with the weight, the difficulty also and hazard of the business, were likewise very unwilling to undertake the managing thereof, and offered an addition of £100 more unto the former sum of £550, that it might not be put upon them.

But being earnestly pressed thereunto by the court, and finding no other means how to set forward that great work, yielded in fine to accept thereof.

Whereupon, soon after, at an assembly of that society, the adventurers entered into a careful consideration how this great and mighty business might, with the most speed and great advantage, be effected.

Whereupon it was agreed and reported by them to employ the said money, together with an addition out of the society's purse of a far greater sum, toward the furnishing out of Captain Bluett and his companions, being so very able and sufficient workmen with all manner of provisions for the setting up of an iron work in Virginia, whereof the profits arising were intended and ordered in a ratable proportion to be faithfully employed for the educating of thirty of the infidels' children in Christian religion, and otherwise as the donor had required.

To which end they writ very effectual letters unto Sir George Yeardley, then governor of Virginia, and captain also of Southampton plantation, not only commending the excellence of the work, but also furnishing him at large with advice and direction how to proceed therein, with a most earnest adjuration, and that often iterated in all their succeeding letters, so to employ his best care and industry therein, as a work wherein the eyes of God, angels, and men were fixed. The copy of my letter and direction, through some omission of their officer, was not entered in their book, but a course should be taken to have it recovered.

In answer of this letter they received a letter from Sir George Yeardley, showing how difficult a thing it was at that time to obtain any of their children with the consent and good liking of their parents, by reason of their tenderness of them, or fear of hard usage by the English, unless it might be by a treaty with Opachankano, the King, which treaty was appointed to be that summer, wherein he would not fail to do his uttermost endeavors.

But Captain Bluett dying shortly after his arrival, it was a great setting back of the iron work intended; yet since that time there had been orders to restore that business with a fresh supply, so as he hoped will the gentleman that gave this gift should receive good satisfaction by the faithful account which they should be able and at all times would be ready to give, touching the employment of the said money.

Concerning which Sir Edwin Sandys further said that, as he could not but highly commend the gentleman for his worthy and most Christian act, so he had observed so great inconvenience by his modesty and eschewing of show of vain glory by concealing his name, whereby they were deprived of the mutual help and advice which they might have had by conferring with him; and whereby also he might have received more clear satisfaction with what integrity, care, and industry they had managed that business, the success whereof must be submitted to the pleasure of God, as it had been commended to his blessing.

He concluded that if the gentlemen would either vouchsafe himself or send any of his friends to confer with the said society, they would be glad to apply themselves to give him all good satisfaction. But for his own particular judgment he doubted that neither of the two courses particularized in this last letter, now read in court, would attain the effect so much desired. Now, to send for them into England and to have them educated here, he found, upon experience of those brought by Sir Tho. Dale, might be far from the Christian work intended. Again, to begin with building of a free school for them in Virginia, he doubted, considering that none of the buildings they there intended had yet prospered, by reason that as yet, through their doting so much upon tobacco, no fit workmen could be had but at intolerable rates, it might rather tend to the exhausting of this sacred treasure in some small fabric, than to accomplish such a foundation as might satisfy men's expectations.

Whereupon, he wished again some meeting between the gentleman or his friends and Southampton society, that all things being debated at full, and judiciously weighed, some constant course might be resolved on and pursued for proceeding in and perfecting of this most pious work, for which he prayed the blessing of God to be upon the author thereof; and all the company said Amen.

In the midst of this narration a stranger stepped in, presenting four books, fairly bound, sent from a person refusing to be named, who had bestowed them upon the college in Virginia, being from the same man that gave heretofore four other great books; the names of those he now sent were, viz: a large church Bible, the Common Prayer Book, Ursinus's Catechism, and a small Bible richly embroidered.

The court desired the messenger to return the gentleman that gave them, general acknowledgment of much respect and thanks due unto him.

A letter was also presented from one that desired not as yet to be named, with £25 in gold, to be employed by way of addition to the former contribution towards the building of a free school in Virginia, to make the other sum £125, for which the company desired the messenger to return him their hearty thanks.

Mr. Copland moved that, whereas it was ordered by the last quarter court that an usher should be sent to Virginia, with the first convenience, to instruct the children in the free school there intended to be erected, that forasmuch as there was now a very good scholar whom he well knew, and had good testimony for his sufficiency in learning and good carriage, who offered himself to go for the performance of this service, he therefore thought good to acquaint the court therewith, and to leave it to their better judgment and consideration, whereupon the court appointed a committee to treat with the said party, viz: Mr. Gibbs, Mr. Wroth, Mr. Wrote, Mr. Copland, Mr. Balmford, Mr. Roberts, who are to join herein with the rest of the committee and to meet about it upon Monday next, in the morning about eight, at Mr. Deputy's, and hereof to make report.

On February 27, 1621-'2, the committee's report touching the allowance granted unto the usher of the free school intended in Virginia being read, Mr. Copland signified that the said usher having lately imparted his mind unto him, seemed unwilling to go as usher or any less title than master of the said school, and also to be assured of that allowance that is intended to be appropriated to the master for his proper maintenance.

But it was answered that they might not swerve from the order of the quarter court, which did appoint the usher to be first established, for the better advancement of which action divers had underwritten to a roll for that purpose drawn, which did already arise to a good sum of money, and was like daily to increase by reason of men's affections to forward so good a work. In which respect many sufficient scholars did now offer themselves to go upon the same condition as had been proposed to this party, yet in favor of him, forsomuch as he was specially recommended by Mr. Copland, whom the company do much respect, the court is pleased to give him some time to consider of it between this and the next court, desiring then to know his direct answer, whether he will accept of the place of usher as has been offered unto him. And if he shall accept thereof, then the court have entreated Mr. Balmford, Mr. Copland, Mr. Caswell, Mr. Mollinge, to confer with him about the method of teaching, and the books he intends to instruct children by.

On the thirteenth of March the court, taking into their consideration certain propositions presented unto them by Mr. Copland in behalf of Mr. Dike, formerly commended for the usher's place in the free school intended at Charles city, in Virginia, they have agreed in effect unto his several requests, namely, that upon certificates from the governor of Virginia of his sufficiency and diligence in training up of youth committed to his charge, he shall be confirmed in the place of the master of the said school.

Secondly, that if he can procure an expert writer to go over with him that can withal teach the grounds of arithmetic whereby to instruct the children in matters of account, the company are contented to give such a one his passage, whose pains they doubt not but will well be rewarded by those whose children shall be taught by him.

And for the allowance of one hundred acres of land he desires for his own proper inheritance, it is agreed that after he hath served out his time, which is to be five years at least, and longer during his own pleasure, he giving a year's warning upon his remove, whereby another may be provided in his room, the company are pleased to grant him one hundred acres.

It is also agreed that he shall be furnished with books, first for the school for which he is to be accountable; and for the children the company have likewise undertaken to provide good store of books, fitting for their use, for which their parents are to be answerable.

Lastly, it is ordered that the agreement between him and the company shall, according to his own request, be set down in writing, by way of articles indented.

Upon the same day the following minute was entered on the journal of the company:

"Whereas, Mr. Deputy acquainted the former court with that news he had received by word of mouth, of the safe arrival of eight of their ships in Virginia with all their people and provisions sent out this last summer, he now signified that the general letter has come to his hands, imparting as much as had been formerly delivered, which letter for more particular relations did refer to the letters sent by the George, which he hoped they should shortly hear of.

"Upon declaration of the company's thankfulness unto God for the joyful and welcome news from Virginia, a motion was made that this acknowledgment of their thankfulness might not only be done in a private court, but published by some learned minister in a sermon to that purpose, before a general assembly of the company, which motion was well approved of and thought fit to be taken into consideration upon return of the George, which was daily expected, when they hoped they should receive more particular advertisement concerning their affairs in Virginia."

Early in April, 1622, the following action was taken :

"Forasmuch as the George was now safe returned from Virginia, confirming the good news they had formerly received of the safe arrival of their ships and people in Virginia, sent this last time, it was now thought fit and resolved according to a motion formerly made to the like effect, that a sermon should be preached to express the company's thankfulness unto God for this his great and extraordinary blessing.

"To which end the court entreated Mr. Copland, being present, to take the pains to preach the said sermon, being a brother of the company, and one that was well acquainted with the happy success of their affairs in Virginia this last year.

"Upon which request, Mr. Copland was pleased to undertake it, and therefore two places being proposed where this exercise should be performed, namely, St. Michael's in Cornhill or Bowe church, it was by erection of hands appointed to be in Bowe church, on Wednesday next, being the 17th day of this present month of April, about 4 o'clock in the afternoon, for which purpose Mr. Carter is appointed to give notice of the time and place to all the company."*

In the month of June there sailed from England Leonard Hudson, a carpenter, his wife, and five apprentices, for the purpose of erecting the East India school at Charles city.

The governor and council of Virginia were at the same time informed, that as the company had failed to secure an usher, upon second consideration it was thought good to give the colony the choice of the schoolmaster or usher, if there was any suitable person for the office. If

* The sermon was delivered, and printed in quarto with this title : "Virginia's God be thanked; or, a sermon of thanksgiving for the happie successe of the affaires in Virginia, this last yeare. Published by commandment of the Virginia company. London, 1622.

they could find no one, they were requested to inform them what they would contribute toward the support of a schoolmaster, and they would then again strive to provide "an honest and sufficient man." The letter concludes by saying, "there is very much in this business that we must leave to your care and wisdom, and the help and assistance of good people, of which we doubt not."

On July 3, 1622, the court gave order that a receipt should be sealed for £47 16*s*., which the gentleman mariners had given to the East India Company to be employed in laying the foundation of a church in Virginia.

The court thought fit to make Captain Martin Prim (the captain of the Royal James) a freeman of the company, and to give him two shares of land in regard of the large contribution which the gentlemen and mariners of that ship had given towards good works in Virginia, whereof he was an especial furtherer.

The placing and entertainment of Mr. Copland in Virginia being referred by the former court to the consideration of a committee, they having accordingly advised about it, did now make report of what they had done therein, as followeth, viz:

1. First, they thought fit that he be made rector of the intended college in Virginia for the conversion of the infidels, and to have the pastoral charge of the college tenants about him.

2. In regard of his rectorship, to have the tenth part of the profits due to the college out of their lands and arising from the labors of their tenants.

3. In regard of his pastoral charge, to have a parsonage there erected, according to the general order for parsonages.

And for that it was now further moved that he might be admitted of the council, then it was referred to the former commitee to consider thereof and of some other things propounded for his better accommodation there.

The committee appointed for the college for this present year are the ensuing, viz: Sir Edwin Sandys, Sir John Danvers, Mr. Gibbs, Mr. J. Ferrar, Mr. R. Smith, Mr. Wrote, Mr. Barbor.

The report of the committee touching Mr. Copland's placing and entertainment in Virginia was now read, they having thought fit he be made rector of the intended college there for the conversion of the infidels, and to have the pastoral charge of the college there for the conversion of the infidels, and to have the pastoral charge of the college tenants about him; and in regard of his rectorship, to have the tenth part of the profits due to the college out of the lands and arising from the labors of their tenants; and in respect of his pastoral charge, to have a parsonage there erected according to the general order for parsonages which this court hath well approved of; and have likewise admitted him to be one of the council of Virginia.

The memorable massacre by the savages, in the spring of 1622, was a great obstacle to all educational progress. Among the mutilated bodies of the slain was that of the refined and educated gentleman, George Thorpe, who had the oversight of the college lands and tenants. After the company received intelligence of his death, they made a particular request that George Sandys, the brother of Sir Edwin, a poet and translator of the Metamorphoses of Ovid, then Treasurer of the colony, should take charge of the college interests; and they wrote: "we esteem the college affairs not only a public but a sacred business." After this we know of but one allusion to the college. In 1623, Edward Downes petitioned "that his son Richard Downes, having continued in Virginia these four years, and being bred a scholar, went over in search of preferments in the college there, might now be free to live there of himself, and have fifty acres of land."

One year after the dissolution of the Virginia Company, in 1624, another attempt was made to erect the East India free school. Mr. Caroloff and others were sent over for the purpose, but he seems to have become unpopular. The governor and council, under date of June 15, 1625, write:

"We should be ready with our utmost endeavors to assist the pious work of the East India free school, but we must not dissemble that, besides the unseasonable arrival, we thought the acts of Mr. Caroloff will overbalance all his other sufficiency though exceeding good."

Fuller, in his "Worthies," speaks of another attempt to establish an academy in Virginia by one Edward Palmer. He says, "his plenteous estate afforded him opportunity to put forward the ingenuity, implanted by nature, for the public good, resolving to erect an academy in Virginia. In order whereunto he purchased an island, called Palmer's island unto this day, but in pursuance thereof was at many thousand pounds' expense, some instruments employed therein not discharging the trust reposed in them with corresponding fidelity. He was transplanted to another world, leaving to posterity the monument of his worthy but unfinished intention. This Edward Palmer died in London, about 1625."

Turning to the manuscript records of the Virginia Company, we learn that on July 3, 1622, "Francis Carter passed over sixteen shares of land in Virginia to Mr. Edward Palmer, of the Middle Temple, London, esquire," who may have been the individual referred to by Fuller, and Palmer's island, at the mouth of the Susquehanna, is where Clayborne traded with the Indians before Lord Baltimore obtained a grant for Maryland.

Although unforeseen circumstances prevented Copeland's acceptance of the rectorship of the proposed college at Henrico, he continued to feel an interest in the American plantations. The leading men of the Virginia Company were also members of the Somers Island or Bermudas Company, and under the auspices of the latter Copeland became a non-conformist minister at those isles of the sea.

Since 1615 the Rev. Richard Norwood, a distinguished surveyor and Puritan, had taught school there, and old records show that both Copeland and Ferrar were contributors to the free school in that locality.

Norwood continued as school teacher for more than thirty years, and in 1648 Copeland, when nearly eighty years of age, accompanied Governor Sayle to establish a new plantation at Eleuthera, one of the Bahamas. In the charter of the colony it was stipulated that each settler should enjoy entire freedom of conscience.

Sayle, shortly after he reached Eleuthera, visited the Puritan parishes of Virginia, and invited the parishioners, who were uncomfortable under the strictness of Governor Berkeley, to remove to the new colony.

The Rev. Mr. Harrison, formerly Berkeley's chaplain, but now a Puritan, was sent to Boston to ask the advice of the ministers there relative to emigration to Eleuthera. They decided that it was inexpedient, partly because an entire separation of church and state was proposed by the projectors of the new settlement. From this period we can learn nothing of Copeland, and probably this early friend of education in America died at the Bahamas.

Four years before John Harvard, the gentle minister of Charlestown, died, and bequeathed his estate to the college at Cambridge, Massachusetts, Benjamin Symmes, of Virginia, left the first legacy by a resident of the American plantations for founding a school. In a will, made in 1634, he gave two hundred acres on the Poquoson, a small stream that enters Chesapeake bay below Yorktown, "with the milk and increase of eight cows, for the maintenance of a learned and honest man, to keep upon the said ground a free school, for the education and instruction of the children of the adjoining parishes of Elizabeth City and Kiquotan, from Mary's Mount downwards, to the Poquoson river."

The author of a little pamphlet on Virginia, published in 1649, alludes to the early friend of education in this language: "I may not forget to tell you that we have a free school, with two hundred acres of land, a fine house upon it, forty milch kine, and other accommodation to it. The benefactor deserveth perpetual mention, Mr. Benjamin Symmes, worthy to be chronicled. Other petty schools we have."

A long period now elapsed before another benefaction to schools was chronicled. Dr. Gataker, in a work dedicated to Oliver Cromwell, and published in 1657, deplores the neglect of education in Virginia. In March, 1660–'1, the assembly of the colony enacted: "That for the advance of learning, education of youth, supply of the ministry, and promotion of piety, there be land taken upon purchase for a college and free school, and that there be, with as much speed as may be convenient, houseing erected thereon for entertainment of students and scholars;" and at the same session a petition to the King was drawn up, praying for "letters patent to collect and gather the charity of well disposed people in England, for the erecting of colleges and schools." The year after the restoration of Charles the Second, a pamphlet, dedicated to the Bishop of London, written by a minister who had lived many years in America, was published, called "Virginia's Cure, or an Advisive Narrative Concerning Virginia," in which it was suggested that charitable persons in England should endow Virginia fellowships in the universities of Oxford and Cambridge. He stated that schools in the colony were so few that "there was a very numerous generation of Christian children born in Virginia, unserviceable for any employment of church or state;" and also adds that the members of the House of Burgesses were "usually such as went over servants thither, and though by time and industry they may have obtained competent estates, yet by reason of their poor and mean condition were unskilful in judging of a good estate, either of church or commonwealth, or of the means of procuring it."

Berkeley, who had been deposed from the governorship during the Cromwellian era, was reinstated in 1661, and proved more churlish than before. In 1671, the home government made a number of queries, the last of which was: "What course is taken about instructing the people within your government in the Christian religion; and what provision is there made for the paying of your ministry?" To which he answered: "The same course that is taken in England out of towns; every man, according to his ability, instructing his children. We have forty-eight parishes, and our ministers are well paid, and by my consent would be better, if they would pray oftener and preach less. But, as of all other commodities, so of this, the worst are sent us, and we had few that we could boast of, since the persecution in Cromwell's tyranny drove divers worthy men hither. But, I thank God, there are no free schools, nor printing, and I hope we shall not have these hundred years; for learning has brought disobedience, and heresy, and sects, into the world, and printing has divulged them and libels against the best government."

Notwithstanding this splenitive declaration of the aged governor, in 1675 Henry Peasley bequeathed six hundred acres in Abingdon parish, Gloucester county, "together with ten cows and one breeding mare, for the maintenance of a free school forever, to be kept with a schoolmaster for the education of the children of the parishes of Abingdon and Ware."

About the period of the accession of William and Mary, a new element in the emigration to Virginia appeared. They were men of angular manners and brawny frames, but also of educated minds and warm hearts. They had been nurtured in a land which for more than a hundred years had enacted in solemn assembly that there should be a school in every parish, for the instruction of youth in grammar, the Latin language, and the principles of religion; and at a later period that the school should be so far supported by the public funds as to render education accessible to even the poorest in the community. Macaulay, in his History of England, referring to the school law of Scotland, says the effect of its passage was immediately felt: "Before one generation passed away it began to be evident that the common people of Scotland were superior in intelligence to the common people of any other country in Europe. To whatever land the Scotchman might wander, to whatever calling he might betake himself, in America or India, in trade or in war, by the advantage which he derived from his early training, he was raised above his competitors."

When these men, bearing the names of Gordon, Monro, Inglis, Irvine, Blair, Porteus, the ancestor of a bishop of the church of England, came to Virginia, there was a stirring of life in communities long torpid. They felt that they had no home unless they had a school-house near, and began anew to agitate the subject of establishing the free school and college. The leader of the movement was the Rev. James Blair, a graduate of the University of Edinburgh in 1673, and gifted with the "fervidam vim Scotorum." His projects met with opposition, but he was canny and did not shrink from a good fight; and, after controversy with Sir Edmund Andros, of Connecticut fame, and with the assembly of Virginia, and his brethren of the church, toward the close of the century succeeded in establishing the College of William and Mary, of which, in a sketch of education during the eighteenth century, it is proposed to give a full history. The preamble to the statutes of William and Mary College, published at an early period both in Latin and English, fully states the influences that led to the organization of the institution, with a portion of which we conclude this historical sketch:

"Nowhere was there any greater danger on account of ignorance and want of instruction than in the English colonies of America, in which the first planters had much to do in a country overrun with weeds and briers, and for many years infested with the incursions of the barbarous Indians, to earn a mean livelihood with hard labor. There were no schools to be found in those days, nor any opportunity for good education.

"Some few, and a very few indeed, of the richer sort, sent their children to England to be educated, and there, after many dangers from the seas and enemies, and unusual distempers occasioned by the change of country and climate, they were often taken off by small-pox and other diseases. It was no wonder if this occasioned a great defect of understanding and all sort of literature, and that it was followed with a new generation of men far short of their forefathers, which, if they had the good fortune, though at a very indifferent rate, to read and write, had no further commerce with the muses or learned sciences, but spent their life ignobly with the hoe and spade, and other employments of an uncultivated and unpolished country. There remained still, notwithstanding, a small remnant of men of better spirit, who had the benefit of better education themselves in their mother country, or at least had heard of it from others. These men's private conferences among themselves produced at last a scheme of a free school and college," which was exhibited to the president and council in 1690, a little before the arrival of Lieutenant Governor Nicholson, and the next year to the assembly, when Blair was sent to England to collect funds for the college.

NOTES

ON

AMERICAN HISTORY.

BY

EDWARD D. NEILL.

From the New-England Historical and Genealogical Register for October, 1876.

BOSTON:
DAVID CLAPP & SON, PRINTERS.
1876.

NOTES ON AMERICAN HISTORY.

NOTES ON AMERICAN HISTORY.

No. IX.

English Maids for Virginia Planters.

AMONG the most important measures, inaugurated after Sir Edwin Sandys became the presiding officer of the London Company, was the transportation of virtuous young women to Virginia.

On the 3d of November, O. S., 1619, Sandys at the usual weekly meeting of the Company suggested "that a fit hundred might be sent of women, maids young and uncorrupt to make wives to the inhabitants."

At the regular quarterly meeting held on Wednesday the 17th of the same month he again alluded to the subject. "He understood that the people thither transported, though seated there in their persons for some four years, are not settled in their minds to make it their place of rest and continuance; but having gotten some wealth to return again to England. For the remedying of that mischief and of the establishing a perpetuity of the plantation he advised to send them over one hundred young maids to become wives, that wives, children and families might make them less movable, and settle them together with their posterity in that soil."

First Shipment of Maids.

The first shipment to the number of ninety was made by the "Jonathan" and "London Merchant," vessels which arrived in May, 1620, at Jamestown.

In a circular of the London Company dated July 18, 1620, they declare their intention to send more young women like "the ninety which have been lately sent."

Shipment per "Marmaduke."

In August, 1621, the Marmaduke left the Thames for Virginia with a letter to the Governor, from which we extract the following:

"We send you in this ship one widow and eleven maids for wives for the people in Virginia."

A choice Lot.

"There hath been especial care had in the choice of them for there hath not any one of them been received but upon good commendations, as by a note herewith sent you may perceive."

To be cared for.

"We pray you all therefore in general to take them into your care, and most especially we recommend them to you Mr. Pountes, that at their first landing they may be housed, lodged, and provided for of diet till they be married, for such was the haste of sending them away, we had no means to put provisions aboard, which defect shall be supplied by the Magazine ship. In case they cannot be presently married, we desire they may be put to several householders that have wives, till they can be provided of husbands."

More to come.

"There are near fifty more which are shortly to come, sent by the Earl of Southampton, and certain worthy gentlemen, who taking into their consideration, that the Plantation can never flourish till families be planted, and the respect of wives and children fix the people in the soil, therefore have given this fair beginning."

Price of a Wife.

"For the reimbursing of whose charges, it is ordered that every man who marries one of them gives 120lb weight of best leaf tobacco, and in case any of them die, that proportion must be advanced to make it up, upon those who survive."

Marriage to be Free.

"We pray you to be fathers to them in this business, not enforcing them to marry against their wills; neither send we them to be servants but in case of extremities, for we would have their condition as much better as multitudes may be allured thereby to come unto you. And you may assure such men as marry these women, that the first servants sent over by the Company shall be consigned to them, it being our intent to preserve families and proper married men, before single persons."

The Marmaduke Maids Married.

With the help of an old Virginia muster roll, we have found out that four of the twelve that came in the Murmaduke were married, and alive in 1624.

Maiden.		*Husband.*	*His arrival.*	
Adria	married	Tho's Harris	Ship Prosperous, May,	1610
Anna	"	Tho's Doughty	" Marigold,	1619
Katharine	"	Rob't Fisher	" Elizabeth,	1611
Ann	"	Nich. Bayly	" Jonathan,	1620

Consignment by the "Warwick" and "Tiger."

On Sept. 11, 1621, the London Company again write:

"By this ship [Warwick] and pinnace called the Tiger we also send as many maids and young women as will make up the number of fifty, with those twelve formerly sent in the Marmaduke, which we hope shall be received with the same Christian piety and charity as they were sent from hence."

Price of a Wife raised.

"The providing for them at their first landing and disposing of them in marriage we leave to your care and wisdom to take that order as may most conduce to their good and the satisfaction of the Adventurers for the charges disbursed in setting them forth, which coming to £12 and upwards, they require 150lbs of the best leaf tobacco for each of them. This increase of thirty pounds weight since those sent in the Marmaduke they have resolved to make, finding the great shrinkage and other losses upon the tobacco from Virginia will not bear less."

Extraordinary Care in Selection.

"We have used extraordinary care and diligence in the choice of them, and have received none of whom we have not had good testimony of their honest life and carriage, which together with their names, we send enclosed for the satisfaction of such as shall marry them."

Marriage of "Warwick" Maids.

The following maids were living as wives in 1624, who came in the Warwick.

Maiden.		*Husband.*		*His arrival.*	
Margaret	married	Hezekiah Raughton	in	Bona Nova,	1620
Sarah	"	Edward Fisher	"	Jonathan,	"
Ann	"	John Stoaks			
Ellen	"	Michal Batt	"	Hercules,	1610
Elizabeth	"	Tho's Gates	"	Swan,	1609
Bridget	"	John Wilkins	"	Marigold,	1618
Ann	"	John Jackson	"	Warwick.	

"Tiger" Maids.

The following who came in the Tiger were alive in 1624.

Maid.		*Husband.*		*His arrival.*	
Joan	married	Humphrey Kent	in	"George,"	1619
Joan	"	Tho's Palmer	"		

At a quarterly meeting of the London Company on Nov. 21, 1621, it was mentioned that care had been taken to provide the planters in Virginia with "young, handsome and honestly educated maids," whereof sixty were already sent.

No. X.

The Mayflower People.

The action of the passengers of the Mayflower in forming a social compact before landing at Plymouth Rock seems to have been in strict accordance with the policy of the London Company under whose patent the ship sailed.

On June 9, 1619, O. S., John Whincop's patent was duly sealed by the Company, but this which had cost the Puritans so much labor and money was not used. Several months after, the Leyden people became interested in a new project. On Feb. 2, 1619–20, at a meeting at the house of Sir Edwin Sandys in Aldersgate, he stated to the Company that a grant had been made to John Peirce and his associates. At the same quarterly meeting it was expressly ordered that leaders of particular plantations, associating unto them divers of the gravest and discreetest of their companies, shall have liberty to make orders, ordinances, and constitutions for the better ordering and directing of their business and servants, provided they be not repugnant to the Laws of England.

Five hundred pounds sterling had been presented to the Company for the education of Indian children, and it had been proposed by Sir John Wolstenholme, that John Peirce and his associates might have the training of some of these children, but on the 16th of February a Committee reported "that for divers reasons they think it inconvenient. First, because after their arrival they will be long in settling themselves: As also, that the Indians are not acquainted with them, and so they may stay four or five years before they have account that any good is done."

Under the Peirce patent the Mayflower sailed in September, 1620. She did not return to England until May, 1621. The next month John Peirce and associates took out a new patent from the "Council of New England." In view of this action on July 16th, at a meeting of the London Company, "It was moved seeing that Mr. John Peirce had taken a patent of Sir Ferdinando Gorges, and thereupon seated his company within the limits of the Northern Plantations as by some was supposed, whereby he seemed to relinquish the benefit of the patent he took of this Company, that therefore the said patent might be called in, unless it might appear he would begin to plant within the limits of the Southern Colony."

From this minute it would seem as if Peirce had some understanding with Gorges, in view of the profits from fishing, of settling the Leyden people beyond the confines of the territory of the London Company, although he did not until June 1, 1621, receive a patent from the "Council of New England."

No. XI.

Transportation of homeless London Children.

Sir George Bowles or Bolles, the Lord Mayor of London, and the Aldermen thereof in 1617, "fearing lest the overflowing multitude of inhabitants should, like too much blood, infect the whole city with plague and poverty," devised as a remedy, the transportation to Virginia of their overflowing multitude, and in 1618–19 one hundred children were sent to Virginia.

The next year, 1619, the Mayor Sir William Cockaine resolved to ease the city of many that were ready to starve, and conferred with the Virginia Company. The following memorial from the Company was presented to the Mayor and Aldermen.

"The Treasurer and Company of Virginia assembled in their great and general Court, the 17th of November, 1619, have taken into consideration, the continual great forwardness of this honourable City, in advancing the plantation of Virginia, and particularly in furnishing one hundred children this last year, which by the goodness of God have safely arrived (save such as died on the way) and are well pleased we doubt not, for this benefit, for which your bountiful assistance we in the name of the whole Plantation, do yield unto you deserved thanks.

"And forasmuch as we have resolved to send this next spring very large supplies for the strength and increasing of the Colony styled by the name of the London Colony, and find that the sending of these children to be apprenticed hath been very grateful to the people, we pray your Lordship and the rest, to renew the like favours and furnish us again with one hundred more for the next spring.

"Our desire is, that we may have them of twelve years old and upward, with allowance of £3 apiece for their transportation, and 40s. apiece for their apparel as was formerly granted. They shall be apprenticed, the boys till they come to 21 years of age; the girls till like age, or till they be married. * * * And so we leave this motion to your honourable and grave consideration."

The City co-operated in procuring the second company of children, but some were unwilling to leave London, as the following letter of Sir Edwin Sandys, the presiding officer of the Company, written in January, 1620, N. S., to Sir Robert Naunton, one of the King's Secretaries, indicates.

"The City of London have appointed one hundred children from the superfluous multitude to be transported to Virginia, there to be bound apprentices upon very beneficial conditions. They have also granted £500 for their passage and outfit. Some of the ill-disposed, who under severe masters in Virginia may be brought to goodness, and of whom the City is especially desirous to be disburdened, declare their unwillingness to go. The City wanting authority to deliver, and the Virginia Company to transport these children against their will, desire higher authority to get over the difficulty."

The necessary authority was granted, and the second company of children duly shipped.

In April, 1622, it was proposed to send a third company, but no data can be found to show that they sailed.

No. XII.

Ships arriving at Jamestown, from the Settlement of Virginia until the Revocation of Charter of London Company.

It must always be regretted that the London Company did not keep a proper ship and passenger register. The good Nicholas

Ferrar, Dep. Gov. of the Company, on Oct. 23, 1622, alluded to the errors of management in the transportation of persons and goods. He alluded to ships now going from London and other parts, and that "there was no note or register kept of the names of persons transported whereby himself and other officers were not able to give any satisfaction to the persons that did daily and hourly enquire after their friends gone to Virginia."

The following list of vessels, made up from various sources, although not complete, approaches to accuracy, and is submitted for correction.

Ships which arrived at Jamestown.

1607—1624.

Year.	Mo.	Ship.	Remarks.
1607	April	Susan Constant[1] 100 Tons	Capt. Chris. Newport, 71 passengers
"	"	God Speed 40 "	" Bart. Gosnold, 52 "
"	"	Discovery 20 "	" John Ratcliffe, 20 "
1607–8	Jan'y	John and Francis[2]	" Newport, 50 colonists
1608	April	Phœnix[3]	" Nelson, 70 "
"	Oct.	Mary Margaret	" Newport, 60 "
1609	July	Discovery[4]	" Robt Tindal, Factor Sam. Argall
"	Aug.	Diamond	" Ratcliffe, Gates & Somers Fleet
"	"	Falcon	" Martin, Nelson Master
"	"	Blessing	" Archer, Adams "
"	"	Unity	" Martin, Pett "
"	"	Swallow[5]	" Moore
"	"	Virginia[6]	" Davies, Built in 1607 at Sagadahoc
1610	May	Deliverance 70 tons[7]	Built at Bermudas, and brought
"	"	Patience 30	Gates and Somers with 100 colonists
"	June	Delaware	Lord Delaware's fleet
"	"	Blessing	" " "
"	"	Hercules	" " "
"	Oct.	Dainty	Brought 12 men, 1 woman, 2 or 3 horses
1611	April	Hercules	" 30 colonists
"	May	Elizabeth	Dale's fleet
"	"	Mary and James	" "
"	"	Prosperous	" "
"	Aug.	Star[8]	Gates "
"	"	Swan	" "
"	"	Trial	" "
"	"	Three Carvills	" "

[1] The Susan Constant, Capt. Newport, left Jamestown for England with mineral and forest specimens on 22 June, 1607, and arrived in the Thames in less than five weeks.

[2] Loaded with iron ore, sassafras, cedar posts, and walnut wood, sailed from Jamestown 10th of April, and on 20th of May reached England. The iron ore seems to have been smelted, and 17 tons sold to East India Co. at £4 per ton.

[3] Capt. Nelson returned to England in July, 1608.

[4] Discovery brought no passengers nor supplies, but was intended for private trade.

[5] Twenty-eight or thirty were sent in ship Swallow to trade for corn with the Indians. They stole away with what was the best ship, and some became pirates. Others returned to England and told the tragical story of a man at Jamestown so pinched with hunger as to eat his dead wife.—See *Purchas*, vol. iv. p. 1757.

[6] This vessel was built at Sagadahoc by the Popham colonists in 1607. Disheartened by Popham's death they set sail for England in a ship from Exeter, "and in the new pynnace the Virginia."—*Hakluyt Pub.*, vol. vi. p. 180

[7] The Deliverance was built by Richard Frobisher.—See *New-Eng. Hist. and Gen. Reg.*, vol. xxviii. p. 317, for a sketch of this shipwright.

[8] In the autumn of 1611 the Star, of 300 tons, sailed from Jamestown for England with forty fair and large pines for masts.—*Hakluyt Pub.*, vol. vi. p. 130.

1612	——	John and Francis	A small ship
"	——	Sarah	" " "
"	Sept.	Treasurer	Capt. Argall, 50 men
1613		Elizabeth	Brought thirteen persons
1614		"	Second trip
1615		John and Francis	Brought twenty persons
"		Treasurer	" " "
1616	Oct.	Susan	Came in October laden with supplies
1617	May	George[1]	Gov. Argall and Rev. Mr. Keith, passengers
		Pinnace	Owned by Capt. Martin
1618	April	George	
		Diana	
"		Sampson	
"	Aug.	Neptune	Lord Delaware died on the voyage; among the passengers Wm. Ferrar who settled Ferrar's Island
		Treasurer	Capt. Elfred, Gov. Argall part owner
1619	March	Wm. and Thomas[2]	Probably the vessel in which Blackwell and other puritans sailed
"	April	Eleanor	Swift pinnace in which Argall secretly escaped
"	"	Gift	Gov. Yeardley passenger. 14 persons died on the voyage
"	May	George	
"		Duty	
"		Prosperous	
"		Marigold	
"		Edwin	
"	June	Trial	
"	Aug.	Privateer[3]	Commissioned by Duke of Savoy, consort of Treasurer, brought "20 negars"
"	Nov.	Bona Nova[4]	Of 200 tons. Brought Rev. Jonas Stockton, son and 120 colonists

[1] In April when the George arrived the number of men, women and children in Virginia was about 400, "and but one plough was going in all the country."—*Sir Edwin Sandys to Virginia Company.*

[2] The "William and Thomas" was without doubt the vessel in which the first body of Puritans embarked under Blackwell, formerly an Elder in the Amsterdam Church.

In Bradford's History, Cushman the Agent of the Leyden people writes under date of London, May 8, 1619, as follows: "Captain Argol is come home this week, * * * came away before Sir Geo. Yeardley came there. * * * He saith Mr. Blackwell's ship came not there till March, but going towards winter they had north-west winds which carried them to the southward beyond their course. And the master of the ship and some six of the mariners dying, it seemed they could not find the Bay till after long seeking and beating about. Mr. Blackwell is dead, and Mr. Maggner the captain; yea, there are dead he saith 130 persons one and other in that ship; it is said there were in all 180 persons in the ship, so as they were packed together like herrings. They had amongst them the flux, and also the want of fresh water, so as it is here rather wondered at that so many are alive, than that so many are dead. The merchants here say it was Mr. Blackwell's fault to pack so many in the ship."

[3] The Treasurer with a commission as privateer from the Duke of Savoy against the Spaniards left Virginia on a cruise to the West Indies, where she consorted with the Flemish ship, and captured a Spanish vessel with some negroes. The Flemish ship brought twenty negroes to Virginia in August, 1619, the first introduced.

On February 16, 1623–4, there had been but a small increase.

At Fleur Dieu Hundred	11	negroes
" James City	3	"
" James Island	1	"
" Plantation opposite	1	"
" Warasquoyak	4	"
" Elizabeth City	1	"
	21	

[4] The Bona Nova with the seven ships that follow in the list brought out 871 persons. *Hist. Virginia Co. of London*, p. 181.

1620	May	Duty	Of 70 tons, Capt. Damyron, brought 50 Bridewell vagabonds
"	"	Jonathan[1]	Of 350 tons. Brought maids for planters' wives
"	"	Trial	Of 200 tons, Capt. Edmonds, 60 kine, 40 persons
"		Falcon	Of 150 tons, Capt. Jones, 4 mares, 52 kine, 36 persons
"		London Merchant	Of 300 tons, Capt. Shaw, 200 persons
"		Swan	" 100 " brought 71 persons
"	Nov.	Francis Bona Ventura[2]	" 240 " " 151 " Rev. David Sandis passengers
1621	Jan'y	Supply	
"		Abigail	
"		Adam	
"		Margaret and John	
"		Bona Nova[3]	
		Charles	
"	Oct.	George	Gov. Wyatt, Rev. Haut Wyatt, Dr. Pott, George Sandys, poet, passengers
		Eleanor	
		Sea Flower	Rev. W. Bennett, passenger
		Concord	
		Duty	
"	Nov.	Marmaduke	Capt. John Dennis, brought for wives, 1 widow and 11 maids
		Flying Hart[4]	Capt. Cornelius Johnson, a Dutchman, brought cattle of Daniel Gookin from Ireland
"	Dec.	Temperance	
		Warwick	This ship and the Tiger brought 38 maids for wives
		Tiger[5]	Captured by Turks and released

[1] The Jonathan was a supply ship, and was among the first to bring maids for wives. On Nov. 3, 1619, Sir Edwin Sandys at a meeting of Virginia Company "wished that a fit hundred might be sent of women, maids young and uncorrupt to make wives to the inhabitants." The girls were sent from time to time, but not in one ship.

[2] On Dec. 16, 1620, Sir Edwin Sandys reported to the Virginia Company "that they had received certificate of the safe arrival of all their ships sent the last Spring, as namely, the Francis Bona Ventura with all save one, the Trial and Falcon with all their passengers, the London Merchant with all theirs, the Duty with all save one. And so likewise the Swan of Barnstable. But the Jonathan, in her tedious passage, had lost sixteen of two hundred. So by this last supply they had landed in Virginia, near the number of 800 persons, for which great blessing, he rendered unto the Almighty all possible thanks."

[3] The ships sent out by the London Company in 1621 were nine in number: the George, Sea Flower, Bona Nova, Concord, Marmaduke, Warwick, Tiger, etc. Upon the return of the "George" in 1622, the Company invited the Rev. Patrick Copland to preach a Thanksgiving Sermon in view of the safe arrival of all their ships at Jamestown. Upon the 18th of April, Copland in accordance with the request preached at Bow Church. Alluding to the vessels he uses these words: "The fittest season of the year for a speedy passage being now far better known than before, and by that means, the passage itself made almost in so many weeks as formerly it was wont to be made in months, which I conceive to be, through the blessing of God, the main cause of the safe arrival of your last fleet of nine sail of ships that not one (but one, in whose room there was another borne) of eight hundred which were transported out of England and Ireland should miscarry by the way."

[4] The Flying Hart brought Daniel Gookin of Ireland, with fifty men of his own, thirty other passengers, and a number of cattle. The London Company writing to the authorities of Virginia under date of Aug. 12, 1621, allude to Gookin. They say: "Let him have very good tobacco for his cows now at his first voyage, for if he make a good return, it may be the occasion of a trade with you from those parts, whereby you may be abundantly supplied, not only with cattle, but with most of those commodities you want at better and easier rate." Clarke seems to have been the pilot of the ship.

[5] The Tiger was captured by the Turks and released. Copland in his sermon alludes to it in these quaint words:

"When God brought some of the ships of your former fleets to Virginia in safety, here God's providence was seen and felt privately by some; and this was a deliverance written as it were on *quarto*, on a lesser paper and letter.

"But now, when God brought all of your nine ships, and all your people in them, in

1622	April	Bona Nova[1]	200 Tons. Capt. John Hudleston
"	"	Discovery[2]	Capt. Thos. Jones
"	July	Charity	Came by way of Plymouth in New England
"		God's Gift	
"		Darling	
		Furtherance	Nathaniel Basse, Passenger
"		Abigail	Catherine, wife of Rev. W. Bennett, Passenger
"		Southampton	
"		James	Rev. Greville Pooley, Passenger
1623	April	Providence[3]	Capt. Clarke, chartered by Daniel Gookin
"		Margaret and John	
"		Sea Flower	
"	July	Samuel	
"		True Love	
"	Aug.	Ann	
"	Oct.	George	
1624		Prosperous	
		Jacob	
		Susan	
		Due Return	Capt. Wm. Peirce

safety and health to Virginia, yea, and that ship Tiger of yours, which had fallen into the hands of the Turkish men-of-war, through tempests and contrary winds she not being able to bear sail, and by that means driven out of her course, some hundreds of miles, * * * * * * * * * When this your Tiger had fallen into the hands of those merciless Turks who had taken from them most of their victuals, and all of their serviceable sails, tackling and anchors, and had not left them so much as an hour-glass, or compass to steer their course, thereby utterly disabling them from going from them; when I say God had ransomed her out of their hands, by another sail which they espied, and brought her likewise safely to Virginia, with all her people, two English boys only excepted, for which the Turks gave them two others, a French youth and an Irish, was not here the presence of God printed as it were in *folio*, on royal crown paper, and capital letters."

[1] Capt. Hudlestone arrived at Jamestown sixteen days after the first great massacre of the whites by Indians. In June, 1622, he was fishing off the coast of Maine, and sent a boat to the Puritans of Plymouth Rock with a letter containing the sad news. He said, "I will so far inform you that myself with many good friends in the Southern Colony of Virginia have received such a blow, that 400 persons large will not make good our losses."—See *Bradford.*

[2] For Sketch of Capt. Jones, see vol. xxviii. p. 314.

[3] Clarke had been captured by the Spaniards in 1612. On June 20, 1620, Cushman writing to his pastor Robinson at Leyden said, "We have hired another pilot here, one Mr. Clarke who went last year to Virginia with a ship of kine."

On Feb. 13, 1621–22, the Presiding Officer of the London Company acquainted them "that one Mr. John Clarke being taken from Virginia long since by a Spanish ship that came to disarm that plantation, forasmuch as he hath since that time done the Company good service in many voyages to Virginia and of late went into Ireland for the transportation of cattle to Virginia, he was an humble suitor that he might be admitted a free brother of the Company."

Soon after he arrived in the "Providence" he died.

EARLY SETTLEMENT

OF

VIRGINIA AND VIRGINIOLA,

AS NOTICED BY

POETS AND PLAYERS

IN THE TIME OF SHAKSPEARE, WITH SOME LETTERS ON THE ENGLISH COLONIZATION OF AMERICA, NEVER BEFORE PRINTED.

By REV. EDWARD D. NEILL, A. B.,

Author of "English Colonization of America," "Virginia Company of London," "Virginia Colonial Clergy," "Terra Mariæ," "Founders of Maryland," "Fairfaxes of England and America," and "History of Minnesota."

MINNEAPOLIS, MINN.:
JOHNSON, SMITH & HARRISON.
1878.

EARLY SETTLEMENT

OF

VIRGINIA AND VIRGINIOLA,

AS NOTICED BY

POETS AND PLAYERS

IN THE TIME OF SHAKSPEARE, WITH SOME LETTERS ON THE ENGLISH COLONIZATION OF AMERICA, NEVER BEFORE PRINTED.

By REV. EDWARD D. NEILL, A. B.,

Author of "English Colonization of America," "Virginia Company of London," "Virginia Colonial Clergy," "Terra Mariæ," "Founders of Maryland," "Fairfaxes of England and America," and "History of Minnesota."

MINNEAPOLIS, MINN.:
JOHNSON, SMITH & HARRISON.
1878.

Virginia and Virginiola.

A PUPIL of Westminster School, in London, one day visited a relative at the Middle Temple, upon whose table were opened books of travel and a map of the world. As distant seas and vast kingdoms but little known were exhibited, the schoolboy resolved, if he ever entered the University, he would pursue geographical studies, and in consequence of the purpose then formed, became Richard Hakluyt, the best authority of his period, in England, relative to the climate, races and productions of the four quarters of the globe.

At the time that Sir Francis Drake was fitting out his expedition for America, he was chaplain to the English Embassy in Paris, and so great was his interest in the project, that he wrote that he was ready to fly to England "with wings of Pegasus," to devote his reading and observation to the furtherance of the work. And after the gallant navigator sailed up the Pacific coast to the fortieth degree north, "the first to loose the girdle of the world, and encompass her in his fortunate arms,"[1] he was delighted in listening to the tales of returning mariners. The Muscovy, Greenland, and other trading companies did not plan expeditions without seeking his advice. In the minutes of the East India Company, under date of January 29, 1601-2, is the following:—"Mr. Hakluyt, the historiographer of the East India Company, being here before the Committees, and having read unto them out of his notes and books, was requested to set down in writing a note of the principal places in the East Indies, and where trade is to be had, to the end that the same may be used for the better instruction of our factors in the said voyage."

1 Purchas's *Pilgrimage*, p. 1779.

2 Cal. of State Papers, East Indies, 1513-1616, p. 120.

On the 14th of May, 1602, Bartholomew Gosnold, a man of integrity, landed from the ship "Concord," with Gabriel Archer and others, on the coast of what is now called Massachusetts, and passed a month in examining the shores, to-day conspicuous with the domes and monuments of Boston, the church spires of peaceful villages, and the tall chimneys of manufacturing towns, and gave to one of its headlands, a name still retained, Cape Cod. Embarking for the return voyage on the 18th of June, he cast anchor in English waters on the 23d of July, and astonished the mercantile world not only by the shortness of his passage by the new route, but by his calm and reasonable statements as to the healthfulness of the region visited, and its capabilities for sustaining an English speaking population.

Prominent among eager listeners to his statement was Hakluyt, then connected with the cathedral at Bristol, who cordially seconded his desire to found a Nova Britannia on the western continent. Many meetings were held by Gosnold and Hakluyt with the Bristol merchants; and Robert Salterne, who had accompanied the former in the voyage to America, was appointed with Hakluyt to obtain permission from Sir Walter Raleigh to make a settlement under his patent.[1] Raleigh's consent obtained, Salterne in 1603 made a second visit with an expedition that left Bristol, who was followed in 1605 by Captain George Weymouth, who returned with several Indians, who remained for more than two years in England.

These successive voyages, under the auspices of the most distinguished and enterprising men of Bristol, Plymouth and London, deepened the conviction that British pride and interests demanded that they should separate the French settlements on the St. Lawrence, and the Spanish plantations near the Gulf of Mexico, by an English colony. The stage is always quick to allude to the absorbing questions of the hour, and in 1605 the play of "Eastward Ho,"[2] in the coarse language of the period, reproduced the conversations

1 Gorges.

2 "Eastward Ho" was the united production of Marston, Chapman and "rare Ben Jonson." Langbaine writes of Chapman, "I can give him no better commendation than that he was so intimate with the famous Johnson as to engage in a triumvirate with him and Marston in a play called 'Eastward Ho.'"

that had taken place on the pavements around the Royal Exchange:—

"*Sea Gull.*—Come, drawer, pierce your neatest hogshead, and let's have cheer, not fit for your Billingsgate tavern, but for our Virginian Colonel; he will be here instantly.

"*Drawer.*—You shall have all things fit, sir; please you have any more wine?

"*Spend All.*—More wine, slave! whether we drink it or no; spill it and draw more.

"*Sea Gull.*—Come, boys, Virginia longs till we share the rest of her maidenhead.

"*Spend All.*—Why, is she inhabited already with any English?

"*Sea Gull.*—A whole country of English is there, man, bred of those left there in '79; they have married with the Indians, and make 'hem bring forth as beautiful faces as any we have in England; and therefore the English are so in love with 'hem that all the treasure they have they lay at their feet.

"*Scapethrift.*—But is there such treasure there, Captain, as I have heard?

"*Sea Gull.*—I tell thee, gold is more plentiful there than copper is with us, and for as much red copper as I can bring I'll have thrice weight in gold. Why, man, all their dripping-pans and chamber-pots are pure gold; and all the chains with which they chain up their streets are massive gold; all the prisoners they take are fettered in gold; and for rubies and diamonds they go forth in holy days and gather 'hem by the sea-shore to hang on their children's coats and stick in their children's caps as commonly as our children wear saffron-gilt brooches and groates with holes in 'hem.

"*Scapethrift.*—And it is a pleasant country withal?

"*Sea Gull.*—As ever the sun shin'd on; temperate and full of all sorts of excellent viands; wild boar is as common there as our tamest bacon is here; venison as mutton. And then you shall live freely there, without sargeants or courtiers, or lawyers or intelligencers. Then for your means to advancement—there it is simple, and not preposterously mixt. You may be an alderman there, and never be a scavenger; you may be any other officer, and never be a slave. You may come to preferment enough, and never be a pander; to riches and fortune and have never the more villany nor the less wit. Besides, there we shall have no more law than conscience, and not too much of either; serve God enough, eat and drink enough, and 'enough is as good as a feast.'"

The statesmen of the day were not indifferent to the enterprise, for since the war with Spain had ceased, the streets of London had been filled with men, who had been soldiers in Ireland and in the Netherlands, averse to return to the quiet peasant life from which they had been pressed into military service, and yet unfitted to obtain a living by honest industry. Too indolent to handle the spade, they were forced to beg or to steal, and became a terror to the peaceable citizen on the side-walk, or the traveller on the highway.

Military officers also favored the scheme, in the hope that the development of a new commonwealth would furnish an occasion for them to draw once more the swords that hung upon the wainscoted walls of their houses, and beginning to rust in the scabbards. Merchants were willing to make pecuniary advances, believing that their money would be returned with interest; and clergymen were eloquent in urging their parishioners to aid in an effort which might lead to the conversion of the savages. Gosnold occupied a whole year in obtaining associates to engage in founding a commonwealth in America, and then a second year in obtaining colonists, and procuring ships and supplies.[1] In answer to a petition to King James, on the 6th of April, 1606, a patent was sealed for Sir Thomas Gates, an officer in the employ of the Netherlands, Sir George Somers, well acquainted with navigation, Richard Hakluyt, who had become Prebendary of Westminster; Edward Maria Wingfield, Bartholomew Gosnold, and others, "to reduce a colony of sundry people into that part of America commonly called Virginia," between the 34th and 45th degrees of north latitude.

The patentees contemplated two plantations. Gates, Somers, Hakluyt, and others, chiefly of London, under the charter, were designated the First Colony, and authorized to settle between the 34th and 41st degrees of north latitude, while Hannam, Gilbert, Parker, Popham, and associates of Plymouth, were called the Second Colony, and permitted to plant between the 38th and 45th degrees of the same latitude.

Early in the winter there was gathered, as a nucleus for a colony, a hundred men, no better than those that surrounded David at the cave of Adullam.

The directions prepared for the first Council of Virginia, by the London Company concludes as follows:

"You must take care that your mariners that go for wages do not mar your trade, for those that mind not to inhabit, for a little

1 Purchas, iv., 1705.

gain will debase the estimation of exchange, and hinder the trade for ever after; and therefore you shall not admit or suffer any person whatsoever, other than such as shall be appointed by the President and Counsel there, to buy any merchandizes, or other things whatsoever.

"It were necessary that all your carpenters, and all other such-like unknown about building, do first build your store-house, and those other rooms of public and necessary use, before any house be set up for any private person; and though the unknown may belong to any private persons, yet let them all work together—first for the Company, then for private men.

"And seeing order is at the same price with confusion, it shall be advisably done to set your houses even, and by a line; that your street may have a good breadth, and be carried square about your market-place, and every street's end opening into it; that from thence, with a few field pieces, you may command every street throughout, which market place you may also fortify, if you think needful.

"You shall do well to send a perfect relation by Capt. Newport[1] of all that is done, what length you are seated, how far into the land, what commodities you find, what soil, woods, and their several kinds, and so of all other things else, to advertise particularly; and to suffer no man to return but by passport from the President and Counsel, nor to write any letter of anything that may discourage others.

"Lastly and chiefly, the way to prosper and achieve good success is to make yourselves all of one mind, for the good of your country and your own, and to serve and fear God, the Giver of all goodness; for every plantation which our Heavenly Father hath not planted shall be rooted out."

Newport was an experienced mariner, and about a year before had returned from the West Indies with a present to King James, who was fond of the rare and curious, of a wild boar and two young crocodiles.

1 A Relation was prepared by Newport, but not published by Purchas, who had examined it. The MS. is in the Lambeth Library, and the Relation was lately, and for the first time, printed by the American Antiquarian Society. It is a fair and accurate description of the first Virginia exploration.

As the hour for the sailing of the expedition arrived, many prayers ascended for its welfare. Scholars, divines, statesmen, merchants, labourers, all classes and conditions of men heartily adopted the sentiment of Drayton's spirited ode called the—

VIRGINIAN VOYAGE.

" You brave, heroic minds,
Worthy your country's name,
That honour still pursue,
Whilst loit'ring hinds
Lurk here at home with shame;
Go, and subdue!

" Britons! you stay too long,
Quickly abroad bestow you;
And with a merry gale
Swell your stretch'd sail,
With vows as strong
As the winds that blow you.

" Your course securely steer,
West and by south, forth keep,
Rocks, lee shores nor shoals,
When Eolus scowls,
You need not fear,
So absolute the deep.

" And cheerfully at sea,
Success you still entice,
To get the pearl and gold,
And ours to hold
Virginia,
Earth's only paradise.

" In kenning the shore,
Thanks to God, first given,
O you, the happiest men,
Be frolic then,
Let cannons roar,
Fighting the wide heaven.

" And in regions far,
Such heroes bring ye forth,
As those from whence we came,
And plant our name
Under that star
Not known to our north.

" And as there plenty grows
Of laurel, everywhere
Apollo's sacred tree,
You, it may see
A poet's brows
To crown, that may sing there.

" Thy voyages attend,
Industrious Hackluit,
Whose reading shall inflame
Men, to seek fame
And much commend
To after time, thy wit."

On the 19th of December the vessels started down the Thames, but owing to the weather, did not sail from the Downs until the 1st of January, 1606–7.

Newport, in command of the fleet, sailed in the "Susan Constant," a ship of one hundred tons, with seventy-one passengers. The zealous promoter of the project, Capt. Bartholomew Gosnold, and fifty-two colonists were in the "Godspeed," a small vessel of fifty tons; and Capt. John Ratcliffe, with twenty others, sailed in the "Discovery," a pinnace of only twenty tons burthen.

Among those who embarked was a quick-witted, illiterate and self-reliant man, John Smith, who in six weeks after they were out of sight of the coast of England, was suspected of a design to lead a mutiny.

On the 26th of April 1607, the expedition entered the broad and beautiful Chesapeake Bay, and that night the sealed orders were opened, and the following persons were designated as members of the Colonial Council: Edward Maria Wingfield, Bartholomew Gosnold, John Smith, Christopher Newport, John Ratcliffe, John Martin and John Kendall. The Council, in accordance with their instructions, soon selected Wingfield, a man of honourable birth and a strict disciplinarian, as their President.[1]

On the 29th a cross was planted at Cape Henry, and the country claimed in the name of King James; and the next day the ships anchored off Point Comfort, now Fortress Monroe. The 1st of May they began cautiously to ascend the James river; and on the 13th landed on a peninsula, in front of which there was good anchorage. All of the Councillors were duly sworn, except Smith, whose conduct during the voyage had been disreputable.

In accordance with the orders prepared at London, Captain Newport, in a shallop, with five gentlemen and nineteen others, explored the river above the site of Jamestown.

At one of the Indian villages, not far from where is now the city of Richmond, they saw a lad ten years of age with yellow hair and light skin, probably the offspring of one of the colonists, left at Roanoke by White, and an Indian concubine.[2] On the 24th of May at the foot of the falls of the James River, Newport planted a cross on which were inscribed his own name and that of King James. On the 26th, a day before the return of the explorers, two hundred

[1] He was the grandson of Sir Robert Wingfield of Huntingdonshire, and the son of Thomas Maria Wingfield, who was thus christened, in compliment to Queen Mary, by Cardinal Pole.—*Camden Society Pub.*, *No.* 43. In 1588 Ferdinando Gorges and Edward Wingfield were prisoners of war at Lisle.

[2] Strachey says: "His Majesty hath been acquainted that the men, women and children of the first plantation at Roanoke, were, by commandment of Powhattan, he persuaded thereto by his priests, miserably slaughtered, without any offence given by the first planted, who twenty and odd years had peaceably lived intermixed with those savages, and were out of his territory.—*Hakluyt Society Pub.*, vol. vi. p. 85.

savages attacked Jamestown, and Wingfield bravely resisted them, being foremost in danger, and an arrow of the enemy passing through his beard.

After they had been nearly a month on shore, on the 10th of June, John Smith was permitted to take the oath of councillor. On Sunday, the 21st, the communion was administered by the devoted Chaplain of the colony, Robert Hunt, and in the evening Newport gave a farewell supper on board of his vessel, and the next day, lifting anchor, sailed, and reached England in less than six weeks by the new and more direct route, bearing the first official communication from an English colony in North America, which is still preserved among the Percy papers with its endorsement in the library of the Earl of Northumberland.

COPPIE OF A LETTER FROM VIRGINIA, DATED 22D OF JUNE, 1607, THE COUNCELL THEIR TO THE COUNCELL OF VIRGINIA HERE IN ENGLAND.

Wee acknowledge our selues accomptable for o^r^ time here spente were it but to giue you satisfaccon of o^r^ industries and affeccons to this moste Ho^ble^ accon, and the better to quicken those good spirritts wch haue alreadie bestowed themselues heere, and to put life into such dead understandings or beleefs that muste firste see and feele the wombe of o^r^ labour and this land before they will entertaine anie good hope of vs or of the land:

W^th^in less than seauen weekes, wee are fortified well against the Indians, we haue sowen good store of wheate, wee haue sent yow a taste of Clappboord, wee haue built some houses, wee haue spared some hands to a discouerie, and still as god shall enhable vs wth strength wee will better and better our proceedinges.

Our easiest and richest comodity being Sasafrax rootes were gathered vpp by the Sailors wth losse and spoile of manie of our tools and w^th^drawing of o^r^ men from our labour to their vses againste our knowledge to our preiudice, wee earnestlie entreat yow (and doe truste) that yow take such order as wee be not in this thus defrauded, since they be all our waged men, yet doe wee wishe that they be reasonablie dealt w^th^all so as all the losse, neither fall on vs nor them. I beleeue they haue thereof two tonnes at the leaste wch if they scatter abroad at their pleasure will pull down our price for a long time this wee leaue to your wisedomes. The land would fflowe wth milke and honey if so seconded by yor carefull wisedomes and bountifull hands, wee doe not perswade to shoote one Arrowe to seeke another but to finde them both. And wee doubt not but to send them home wth goulden heads at leaste our desires, laboures and liues shall to that engage themselues.

Wee are sett downe 80 miles wthin a River, for breadth sweetness of water, length navigable vpp into the country deepe and bold channell so stored wth Sturgion and other sweete Fishe as no mans fortune hath euer possessed the like. And as wee thincke if more maie be wished in a River it will be founde. The soile is moste fruictfull, laden wth good Oake, Ashe, Wallnut tree, Popler, Pine, sweete woodes, Cedar and others yett wthout names that yeald gumes pleasant as Franckumcense, and experienced amongest vs for greate vertewe in healing greene woundes and aches, wee entreat your succours for o^{r} seconds wth all expedition leaste that all deuouringe Spaniard lay his rauenous hands uppon theas gold showing mountains, wch if it be so enhabled he shall neuer dare to thinck one:

This noate doth make known where o^{r} necessities do moste strike vs, we beseech yor present releiffe accordinglie otherwise to o^{r} greatest and laste griefes, wee shall against our willes not will that wch wee most willingly would.

Captaine Newporte hath seene all and knoweth all, he can fullie satisfie your further expectations, and ease you of our tedious letters, wee most humblie praie the heauenly Kings hand to bless o^{r} labours wth such counsailes and helpes as we may further and stronger proceede in this our Kinges and countries service.

James towne in Virginia this 22th of June An^{o} 1607.

Your poore Friends,

EDWARD MARIA WINGFIELD,	BARTHOLOMEW GOSNOLD,
JOHN SMITH,	JOHN RATTCLIFFE,
JOHN MARTINE,	GEORGE KENDALL.

After a speedy voyage from Jamestown, of thirty-seven days, Newport anchored in Plymouth Sound, and the same day wrote a letter, which is also in the Percy manuscripts, with an ancient endorsement:

COPIE OF A LETTER TO Y^{E} LORD OF SALISBYRIE FROM CAPTAINE NEWPORT Y^{E} 29TH OF JULIE, 1607, FROM PLIMOUTH.

Right Ho^{ble}:

My verie good Lo. my duty in most humble wise remembred it maie please yor good L$^{o'p}$ I arrived here in the Sound of Plimouth this daie from the discourie of that parte of Virginia imposed uppon me and the rest of the Colonie for the South parte, in wch wee haue performed o^{r} duties to the uttermost of o^{r} powers. And have discouered into the country near two hundred miles, and a River nauigable for greate Shippes one hundred and fifty miles. The contrie is excellent and very rich in gold and copper, of the gould we haue brought a Say and hope to be wth y^{r} Lo'^{pp} shortlie to show it his Ma^{ty} and the rest of the Lords. I will not deliver the expectaunce and assurance we haue of great wealth but will leaue it to yor Lo$^{p's}$ censure when you see the probabilities. I wish I might have come in person to haue brought theis glad tidings, but my inability of body, and the not having any man to putt in trust with the shippe and that in her maketh me to deferre my coming till winde and weather be fauourable. And so I moste humbly take my leaue.

From Plimouth this 29th of Julie, 1607.

Your L^{ps} most humbly bounden,

CHRISTOPHER NEWPORTE.

On the 18th of August, 1607, a gentleman in London wrote to a friend "that Captain Newport has arrived without gold or silver, and that the adventurers, cumbered by the presence of the natives, had fortified themselves at a place called Jamestown, no graceful name, and doubts not the Spaniards will call it Villiaco. A Dutchman. writing in Latin, calls the town Jacobolis, but George Percy names it James Fort, which we like the best of all, because it comes near Chelmsford."

The low situation of the settlement, with the swamps in the rear, soon produced sickness, and during the summer nearly every day a new grave was dug. On the 22d of August, the man who had projected the expedition, and expended money in its behalf, "that worthy and religious gentleman," Bartholomew Gosnold,[1] was buried,

1 Anthony, a brother, and Anthony, also a relative, perhaps a son, accompanied Captain Gosnold to Virginia.—*London Co. MSS.*

and the saddened survivors manifested their respect by firing volleys of musketry over his remains.

The colonists, disheartened by the loss of their associates, and the discomforts of immigrant life, chafed under the prudent measures and military exactness of Wingfield. In September the members of the Council demanded a larger daily allowance of food, but he refused, because, with strict economy their supplies would last but thirteen and a half weeks. As a precautionary measure, he also withheld the ration from any that had upon any day obtained fresh fish or wild game. The two gallons of sack and aqua vitæ reserved for the sick and sacramental purposes were even coveted by members of the Council. The President says they "longed for to sup up that little remnant, for they had now emptied their own bottles."

As Wingfield would not yield to the clamor of his associates, Ratcliffe, Smith and Martin, they deposed him, and formed a triumvirate. On the 11th of September he was arraigned before them, and Ratcliffe accused him of refusing him a chicken, a penny whittle, a spoonful of beer, and of giving him damaged corn. Martin charged him with calling him an indolent fellow, and Smith alleged that he called him a liar. After this procedure, contrary to all forms of law, he was imprisoned on board of the pinnace.

The colonists soon discovered that it was easier to live by angling, hunting, and roaming with the Indians, than by tilling the earth. The first winter they pursued their own pleasure, and cared little for the interests of the company they had contracted to serve.

On the 10th of December, Captain Smith ascended the Chichahominy to trade with the Indians, and was treated with great respect and kindness by Powhattan,[1] although two colonists, Emery and Robinson, who went with him, were killed by some hostile savages.

Upon his return to Jamestown, Gabriel Archer, who had become a member of the Council, on the 8th of January, 1607–8, placed

1 Smith speaks of this kindness in his *Relation* of 1608, but sixteen years after leaving Virginia he published another narative in which he contradicts his first statement. Honest Fuller, the Historian, whose schoolmaster was Arthur Smith, a relative of the Captain's, in his *Worthies of England*, gives the following opinion of the Captain's last work: "From the Turks in Europe he passed to the Pagans in America, where such his perils, preservations, dangers, deliverances, they seem to *most men above belief*, to *some beyond truth*. Yet we have two witnesses to attest them, the prose and the pictures, *both in his own book*, and it soundeth much to the diminution of his deeds, that he *alone* is the herald to publish and proclaim them."

Smith under arrest for allowing his companions to be killed, but that day Captain Newport again arrived from England, and ordered the release both of Wingfield and Smith.

After recovering from the fatigue of the sea-voyage, Newport explored the Pamunky river, and was "lovingly entertained" by Powhattan. Returning to Jamestown on the 9th of March, he loaded his vessel with cedar, walnut boards, sassafras, and iron ore. On the 10th of April, 1608, with Archer and Wingfield as passengers, he left Virginia, and on the 20th of May arrived in England.

Wingfield, in reply to the complaints made against him, prepared a full statement of his administration in Virginia for the perusal of the London Company. In it he remarks: [1] "To the President's and Council's objections I say that I do know courtesy and civility became a Governor. No penny whittle was ever asked me, but a knife, whereof I had none to spare. The Indians had long before stolen my knife.

"Of chickens I never did eat but one, and that in my sickness. Mr. Ratcliffe had before that time tasted of four or five. I had by my own housewifery bred about thirty-seven, and the most part of them of my own poultry, [of] all which at my coming away I did not see three living. I never denied him, or any other, beer when I had it. The corn was the same which we all lived upon.

"Mr. Smith, in the time of our hunger, had spread a rumor in the colony that I did feast myself and my servants out of the common store, with intent, as I gathered, to have stirred the discontented company against me. I told him privately in Mr. Gosnold's tent that indeed I had caused half a pint of pease to be sodden with a piece of pork of my own provision for a poor old man which, in a sickness whereof he died, he much desired; and said if out of his malice he had given out otherwise, that he did tell a lie.

"It was proved to his face that he begged in Ireland, like a rogue, without a license.

"Mr. Archer's quarrel to me was because he had not the choice of the place for our plantation, because I misliked his laying out

1 Wingfield's discourse had been perused by Purchas, but he was warped in favor of the sentiments of the plausible Smith. It was copied from the manuscript in Lambeth Library, and printed for the first time with Newport's *Relation*, in vol. iv. of American Antiquarian Society's Collections.

of our town in the pinnace, because I would not swear him of the council for Virginia, which neither would I do nor he diserve ; Mr. Smyth's quarrel, because his name was mentioned in the intended and confessed mutiny by Galthropp ; Thomas Wooton, the surgeon, because I would not subscribe to a warrant to the Treasurer of Virginia to deliver him money to furnish him with drugs and other necessaries, and because I disallowed his living in the pinnace, having many of our men lying sick and wounded in our town, to whose dressings by that means he slacked his attendance.

"Of the same men also Capt. Gosnold gave me warning, misliking much their dispositions, and assured me they would lay hold of me if they could."

Newport, in accordance with his written instructions, also made a report of his explorations. The manuscripts of Wingfield and Newport were both known to Purchas, yet were not published in his collection of voyages, probably because Sir Thomas Smith, who had furnished him money to aid in printing his "Pilgrimage," did not approve of their statements.

In the autumn of the year 1608 he completed his third voyage[1] to Jamestown, bringing seventy passengers, among them Francis West, brother of Lord Delaware, Daniel Tucker, and Raleigh Crashaw. He carried back on his return voyage iron ore, which was smelted and sold to the East India Company.[2]

1 For the fourth time he left England for Jamestown with Gates and Somers, but was wrecked at Bermudas, and did not arrive until the 23d of May, 1610, at Jamestown.

On November 8, 1610, Sir Thomas Smith, Sir Maurice Berkeley, Sir George Coffin and the distinguished lawyer, Richard Martyn, styled on his portrait "*Præco Virginiæ ac Parens*," attorney and founder of Virginia, entered a book at Stationers' Hall, praising the soil and climate of Virginia, and confronting scandalous reports.

When Sir Thomas Dale (in 1611) arrived at Jamestown he was much disappointed in the appearance of the country and the prospects of the Colony ; and the authorities of Virginia, in a communication to the London Company, state that "he pulled Captain Newport by the beard and threatened to hang him for that he affirmed Sir Thomas Smith's relation to be true, demanding of him whether it were meant that the people here in Virginia should feed upon trees."

In the autumn of 1611 the ship Star, of 300 tons, fitted and prepared in England, with scupper-holes to take in masts, sailed from Jamestown with forty fine and large pines. In this vessel Newport was probably a passenger. John Chamberlain, of London, on December 18, 1611, writes to Sir Dudley Carleton : "Newport, the Admiral of Virginia, is newly come home." Soon after this he was appointed one of the six Masters of the Royal Navy, and was employed by the East India Company to carry Sir Robert Sherley to Persia. He was then a married man, as that company allowed £24 to his wife during his absence. On the 13th of June, 1613, he was in the ship Expedition at Saldanha, on

2 Strachey in *Hakluyt Society Pub.* vol. vi. and Cal. of State Papers, East Indies, A. D. 1513—1618.

More than three centuries ago an adventurous Spaniard, John Bermudez, espied the collection of islets set in a coral reef, situated in the Atlantic Ocean about six hundred miles from the coast of Carolina.

In the days of Queen Elizabeth, a roving Englishman, Job Hortop, in a "Book of rare travail," declared that near Bermudas he had sight of a sea-monster, which three times showed himself from the middle upwards in shape like a man, and of the complexion of a "mulato," or tawny Indian. An old chronicler wrote: "This island has been accounted an uninhabited pile of rocks and desolate inhabitation for devils, but all the fairies of the rocks are

the coast of Africa. He returned to England in the summer of 1614, and was much commended by his employers for his service to Sir Robert Sherley and explorations of the Persian Gulf.

Before making another voyage to the East Indies Newport requested a salary of £240, but the Company advised him to "rest awhile," and at length he accepted a salary of £120 a year—one half of what he desired.

Captain Thomas Barwick was also emenployed by the company at this time, and a request of Captain Samuel Argall was referred to Newport for consideration.

Before he left Gravesend in January, 1615, the East India Company raised his salary to £180 a year, with the understanding that he was not to trade upon his own account with the people of India, China and Japan.

On the 16th of May, 1617, Newport was at Saldanha ready to sail for Bantam, on the isle of Java.

In January, 1618, the ship Hope, Captain Newport, was cruising in Asiatic seas.

He arrived in August at Bantam, and soon died there. He had but one child, named John. At a meeting of the Virginia Company, of London, held on the 17th of November, 1619, the following minute was made:

"Whereas, the Company hath formerly granted to Captain Newport a bill of adventure for 400 pounds, and his son now desiring order from this court for the laying out of some part of the same, Mr. Treasurer was authorized to write to Sir George Yeardley and the Counsell of State for the effecting thereof."

The land selected was probably called Newport's News. Mrs. Mary Tue, a daughter of Hugh Crouch, an heir and executrix of Lieutenant Richard Crouch, did assign, in 1622, one hundred and fifty acres of lands at "Newport's News" to Daniel Gookin.

Captain Thomas Barwick, who had been in the same fleet with Newport in the East Indies, in 1619, in a fight with the Hollanders near Bantam, gave up the ship Bear, says an old letter, either "out of cowardliness or sincerity of religion." Upon his return to England, in 1620, he was sent to Newgate and then to the Marshalsea.

In the summer of 1622 Barwick, under the London Company, went to Virginia with twenty-five shipwrights to build boats and pinnaces for the use of the Colony. The Governor and Council, in a letter written during the next January, states: "Capt. Barwick and his company at their arrival were accommodated according to their desire in James City, where they have spent their time in housing themselves, and are now working upon shallops. Since his arrival by sickness he hath lost many of his principal workmen, and he himself at present very dangerously sick." His sickness was unto death.

but flocks of birds, and all the devils in the woods are but herds of swine."

Strachey, who was wrecked with Gates, Somers and Newport, speaks of the Bermudas as an Archipelago of many islands, which "seem rent with tempests of thunder, lightning and rain, which threaten in time to drown them all; the storms keep their unchangeable round, winter and summer, rather thundering than blowing."

William Crashaw, the eloquent divine, preacher of the Temple, and father of the poet whom Cowley touchingly eulogized as "poet and saint," in 1613 used this language: "Who did not think till within these four years but that these islands had been rather a habitation of devils than fit for a man to dwell in? Who did not hate the name when he was on land, and shun the place when he was on seas? But behold the misprision and conceits of the world! For time and large experience hath now told us, it is one of the sweetest Paradises that be upon the earth."

Henry Wriothesley, the Earl of Southampton, the last presiding officer of the Virginia Company of London, the first patron and life-long friend of Shakspeare, in a dispatch to King James announcing the arrival of the first colony at the islets, stated "that the Spaniards, dismayed at the frequency of hurricanes durst not adventure there, but call it Dæmoniorum Insulam, and that the English merchants had sent home some amber and seed pearls, which the devils of Bermudas love not better to retain, than the angels of Castile to recover."

To the English speaking world the Bermudas islands have become familiar in consequence of the wreck in A. D. 1609, on a reef, of the ship Sea Venture, on board which, were Sir Thomas Gates, Sir George Somers, and a number of colonists on their way to Virginia. For several days the vessel, like the grain ship in which the Apostle Paul sailed for Rome, was driven about by the winds, "neither sun nor stars appeared, and no small tempest lay on them, and all hope that they thould be saved was taken away."

The ship's seams opened, and from noon on Tuesday until noon on the following Friday, the 28th of July, A. D. 1609, O. S., the men worked the pumps by day and by night, and yet ten feet of water was in the hold. Some in despair went below the hatches, and finding "some good and comfortable waters," drank one to another, and "made themselves ready in the cabin for the mischance of the hour." [1] Sir George Somers, three score years of age, remained undaunted, and for three days and three nights, to use the words of Prospero,

> "Infused with a fortitude from Heaven," [2]

sat, wide-awake, on the poop of the vessel, giving orders and awaiting the decrees of Providence, when he descried land ahead. This unlooked for and welcome intelligence hurried up those who had been in drunken sleep or moaning below the hatches "to look for that they durst not believe." Hoisting every sail, they made toward shore until the ship struck one of the tortuous passages and stood upright between two rocks about one fourth of a mile from the main island of Bermudas.

The wreck of this ship, and the safe deliverance of the rest of the fleet created a deep impression upon the Earl of Southampton, and from him Shakspeare would learn many particulars, as well as from the printed narratives of some of those who were passengers in the vessel. How vividly has the dramatist reproduced the events in the play of the Tempest in the conversation of Prospero and Ariel.

> *Prospero.* Hast thou, Spirit,
> Performed to point, the tempest I bade thee?
> *Ariel.* To every article.
> * * * The fire and cracks
> Of sulphurous roaring, the most mighty Neptune
> Seemed to besiege, and make his bold waves tremble.
> Yea, his dread trident shake.
> *Prospero.* My brave Spirit!
> Who was so firm, so constant, that this coil
> Would not infect his reason?
> *Ariel.* Not a soul
> But felt a fever of the mad, and played
> Some tricks of desperation; all but mariners,
> Plunged in the foaming brine and quit the vessel.
> * * * * * *

1 Tempest, Act 1, Scene 1.

2 Tempest, Act 1, Scene 2.

Prospero. But was not this nigh shore?
Ariel. Close by, my master.
Prospero. But are they, Ariel, safe?
Ariel. Not a hair perish'd;
On their sustaining garments not a blemish,
But fresher than before * * *
Prospero. Of the king's ship
The mariners, say how thou hast disposed,
And the rest of the fleet?
Ariel. Safely in harbor
Is the king's ship; in the deep nook where once
Thou call'dst me up at midnight to fetch dew
From the still vex'd Bermoothes, there she's hid:
The mariners all under hatches stow'd;
Whom with a charm join'd to their suffer'd labour
I have left asleep; and for the rest o' the fleet,
Which I dispers'd, they all have met again. [1]

It rejoiced Gates, Somers and Newport that, while the ship was a loss, there was no loss of life. Their residence from August to the following May on the Island, was a succession of surprises. What superstitious sailors had asserted were harsh voiced monsters, proved to be grunting hogs, the offspring of black swine that years before had found their way to shore from some Spanish wreck. Fish eagerly leaped upon the hooks placed in the waters; the birds with beautiful plumage and the simplicity of little children hovered around or rested upon the shoulders of the castaways. The palmetto tree furnished food, and its broad leaves were used in constructing light cabins.

Each morning and evening, at the ringing of a bell, the whole company assembled to listen to the prayers according to the order of the Church of England, read by the good Chaplain, Richard Buck. In this "wilderness of sweets" amid the "voiceful music of the sea," Thomas Powell, the cook of Sir George Somers, was lifted above the atmosphere of pots and pans and inspired to tell his love to Elizabeth Persons, a servant-maid of a Mistress Horton, and took her to his wedded wife "for better, for worse, for richer, for poorer, in sickness and in health." Godsips or gossips were busy over the birth of a boy christened Bermudas, and of a girl who received the

1 Tempest, Act 1, Scene 2.

name of Bermuda. At the baptizing of the latter, Captain Newport and Strachey, afterwards secretary of Lord Delaware, stood, says an old chronicler, as "witnesses." Bermuda just peeped into the world, and then went to a "better land," but is deserving of mention, as the daughter of John Rolfe and his white wife—the same John Rolfe who by a wonderful alchemy appears in American history as a devout unmarried young Englishman, praying earnestly for the conversion of Pocahontas, marrying her, says Hamor, "of rude education, manners, barbarous and cursed generation, merely for the good and honor of the Plantation," but in the matter-of-fact transactions of the London Company for A. D. 1622 is spoken of as John Rolfe, lately deceased, with a surving widow and children, besides "a child had by Powhattan's daughter." [1]

Among the company was also Richard Frobisher, an experienced ship carpenter, who afterwards was employed by the East India Company, and lived for a time at Malacca with his wife and two sons. Under his guidance two cedar vessels, the Deliverance, of seventy tons, and the Patience, of thirty tons, were built, their beams fastened together by wooden pegs, and their seams rendered tight by a smearing of lime made from shells, and oil extracted from fish or swine. Upon a palmetto tree near the ship-yard was a Latin inscription, dated May 10th, 1610, the time they sailed from the island, which stated that a ship had been built by Frobisher to transport the castaways to Virginia. It was in these words:

"Conditur, in hoc loco, per Ricardum Frobisherum, quæ Virginiæ nos omnes hinc transportabit."

The portion of the tree upon which this statement was, in 1671 was an honored relic, and hung in the hall of the Governor of Bermudas.

Strachey, in his narrative, mentions another monument which was set up in these words:

"Before we quitted our old quarter, and dislodged to the water, with our pinnasse, our Gouernor set up in Sir George Summers'

1 The following is from the transactions of that company under date of October 7th 1622: "Mr. Henry Rolfe in his petition desiring the estate of his brother John Rolfe, deceased, left in Virginia, might be enquired out for the maintenance of his relict wife and children, and for his indemnity in rearing up the child his said brother had by Powhattan's daughter, is yet living and in his custody."

garden, a faire Mnemosynon in figure of a crosse, made of the timber of our ruined shippe, which was screwed in with strong and great trummels to a mightie cedar, which grew in the middest of the said garden, and whose top and upper branches he caused to be lopped, that the violence of the winds and weather might have less power ouer her.

"In the middest of the crosse ovr Gouernor fastened the picture of his Maiestie, in a piece of silver of twelve pence, and on each side of the crosse, he set an inscription, graven in copper, in the Latine and English to this purpose : In memory of our great deliverance, both from a mightie storm and leake, we haue set vp this to the honour of God. It is the spoyle of an English ship of three hundred tunne, called the Sea Venture, bound with seven ships more, from which the storm divided vs, to Virginia, or Nova Britannia, in America."

When Gates and Somers and Newport with their fellow passengers embarked for Virginia, two persons remained on the island who were fugitives from justice, Edward Waters and Christopher Carter.

The Deliverance and the Patience arrived at Jamestown on the 23d of May, and when Sir George Somers found that the colonists were famishing and feeding upon frogs, "the good old gentleman out of his own love and zeal," says a dispatch of Lord Delaware to the authorities in England, "not motioning but most cheerfully and resolutely" re-embarked in his little cedar pinnace of thirty tons, for the Bermudas, to procure a supply of black hogs there so numerous. While there he died from eating too much of the meat which he had hoped to have carried to the colonists of the James River. His kinsman and fellow passenger, but not his heir, as has been stated, Matthew Somers betrayed his trust, and persuaded all the crew but one, Edward Chard, to sail direct to England.

There were now three human beings left as companions for the birds, and they enjoyed at first their lonely residence, feeling that they were "monarchs of all they surveyed." Each could appreciate the language of Gonzalo in the Tempest :[1]

1 Act 2, Scene 1.

Had I a plantation of this isle, my Lord,
* * * * *
No name of magistrate ;
Letters should not be known ; no use of service,
Of riches, or of poverty ; no contracts,
Successions ; bound of land, tilth, vineyard, none ;
No use of metal, corn, or wine, or oil ;
No occupation ; all men idle, all."

Time was wiled away in prying into crannies and crevices of the coral reefs constructed by millions of polypi, and one day they stumbled upon a mass of ambergris, weighing many pounds. Prosperity did not increase the happiness of the triumvirate ; the golden age began to vanish with the discovery of treasure ; each urged claims which to the others seemed unreasonable ; Chard and Waters quarreled, called each other hard names, and were about to fight a duel, when Carter had a happy thought, and hiding their weapons, enforced peace.

Matthew Somers gave a glowing description of the Bermudas when he returned home, and urged its occupancy. He declared that it was not an isle of devils ; in language resembling Caliban's, he asserted :[1]

"The isle is full of voices,
Sounds, and sweet airs, that give delight, and hurt not.
Sometimes a thousand twanging instruments
Will hum about mine ears ; and sometimes voices
That if I then had wak'd after long sleep,
Will make me sleep again ; and then in dreaming
The clouds methought would open, and shew riches
Ready to drop upon me."

But the merchants of London classed his stories with the travelers' tales—

"That there are unicorns ; that in Arabia
There is one tree, the phœnix throne ; one phœnix
At this hour reigning there."[2]

Virginia had been so highly extolled in the days of Raleigh's attempt to colonize America that the stage players often brought down the house by some allusion to the New World.

1 Tempest, Act 3, Scene 2.

2 Act 3, Scene 3.

The stage caricatures of Virginia were an annoyance to those interested in planting of an English civilization there, and Crashaw in a sermon preached February 21st, 1609–10 in one of the London churches before the stockholders of the Virginia Company and Lord Delaware, the Governor-General elect of the colony, pours out the following invective:

"As for players, pardon me right honorable and beloved for so wronging this place and your patience with so base a subject; they play with princes and with potentates, magistrates and ministers, nay, with God and religion, and all holy things; nothing that is good, excellent, or holy can escape them; how, then, can this nation? But this may suffice that they are players; they abuse Virginia, but they are players; they disgrace it, but they are but players; and they have played with better things, and such for which if they repent not vengeance awaits them.

"But let them play on; they make men laugh on earth, but He that sits in heaven laughs them to scorn, because, like the fly, they so long play with the candle, till first it singes their wings, and at last burns them altogether.

"But why are the players enemies to the plantation? I will tell you the cause; first, for that they are multiplied here that one cannot live by another, and they see that we send all trades to Virginia, but will send no players, which if we would do, those that remain would gain the more at home."

In September, 1610, Sir Thomas Gates and Captain Christopher Newport arrived in London and corroborated the statements concerning the Bermudas, and only a few months later Lord Delaware came back; and an Indian boy who was brought to England by his order, at this time attracted attention as he walked the streets, and perhaps Shakspeare saw him and was led to place these words in Trinculo's mouth.

"What have we here, a man or a fish? Dead or alive? A fish, he smells like a fish; a very ancient and fishlike smell; a kind of, not of the newest Poor John. A strange fish! Were I in England now, (as once I was) and had but this fish painted, not a holiday fool there but would give a piece of silver: then would this monster make a man; any strange beast there makes a man. When they will not give a doit to relieve a lame beggar, they will lay out ten to see a dead Indian."[1]

[1] Act 2, Scene 2, of Tempest.

Early in the year 1612, members of the Virginia Company of London sent an expedition to Virginiola as Bermudas was first called but soon changed to Summer Islands, in respect of the mild, unvarying temperature, and also in remembrance of Sir George Somers. In April of this year the three dwellers on the island were filled with joy at the sight of an approaching ship with the flag of England, which proved to be the Plough with a party of colonists under a Governor More.

"As soon as we landed," says one of the passengers, "we went to prayer, and gave thanks unto the Lord for our safe arrival, and whilst we were at prayer we saw three men coming down to us." Another wrote: "The climate I hold to be very good, and agreeable with our constitution of England, for the men which were left there are very fat and fair, not tanned nor burned in the sun, so much as we."

Chard, one of the trio, being asked by Governor More as to the discovery of ambergris, denied any knowledge, and secretly made an arrangement with the captain of the Plough to have the lump conveyed to England. Carter at length disclosed the plan and confessed that they had the treasure, when Chard was arrested, but was subsequently released, and Governor More in behalf of those he represented, received one-third of the ambergris.

In a few weeks the ambergris was offered for sale in London, and the East India Company bought of the Virginia Company two boxes at sixty-two and sixty-three shillings an ounce. Children stopped at the windows of jewellers' to look at the ornaments made of Bermudas' products; and exclaim, in substance, as in later years the poet Pope:

> "Pretty! in amber to observe the forms
> Of hairs, or straws, or dirt, or worms."

Chapman, the dramatist, wrote a piece which was played by members of Lincoln's Inn, and the Middle Temple, in February, 1613, at the White Hall Palace, London, in honor of the marriage of Frederick, the Prince Palatine, and the Princess Elizabeth, the daughter of King James. The chief maskers were dressed as Indians, with vizards of olive color, feathers on their heads, and long black hair down their shoulders. On the stage was an Island of rocks and caves, and Plutus, Prince of the Virgin land, was prominent. One of the maskers speaks as follows: "A rich island lying in the South Sea, called Pœana, being for strength and riches called the ravel of the South Sea, is by earth's round motion moved near this Britain shore, in which island, being yet in command of the Virginian continent, a troupe of the noblest Virginians, attended hither the God Riches all triumphantly shining in a mine of gold. For hearing of the most royal solemnity of these nuptials they crossed the ocean in their honour and are here arrived."

John Rolfe, soon after his arrival in Virginia from Bermudas, opened the first tobacco plantation, in English North America, and others followed, until Virginia tobacco became known in London stores. In a debate in the House of Commons early in 1614 a member said: "The shop-keepers sent over all kinds of goods, for which they received tobacco instead of wine, infinitely to the prejudice of the Commonwealth. Many of the divines now smell of tobacco, and poor men spend 4d. of their day's wages, at night, in smoke."

In the Mask of Flowers, performed at White Hall on Twelfth Night, 1612–13, by gentlemen of the Inner Temple and Gray's Inn, under the auspices of Sir Francis Bacon, afterwards Lord Verulam, and others. Silenus challenges Kawasha, the God of the Florida Indians, and declares that wine is more worthy of praise than tobacco. Kawasha was personated by a masker with a cap of red cloth of gold, pendants in his ears, a glass chain about his neck; his body and legs covered with olive colored cloth, and in his hand a bow and arrows, and "the bases of tobacco colored stuff cut like tobacco leaves." The colloquy is spirited and well sustained:

Silenus. "Kawasha comes in majestic,
Was never such a God as he:
He's come from a farre countrie
To make our nose a chimney.

Kawasha. The Wine takes the contrary way
To get into the hood,
But good Tobacco makes no stay

But seizeth where it should.
More incense hath burned at
Great Kawashae's foote
Than to Silen and Bacchus both,
And take in Jove to boote.

Silenus. The Worthies they were nine, 'tis true,
And lately Arthur's Knights I knew,
But now are come up Worthies new,
The roaring boys, Kawashae's crew.

Kawasha. Silenus toppes the barrel, but
Tobacco toppes, the braine
And makes the vapours fire and soote,
That man revives againe—
Nothing but fumigation
Doth charm away ill spirits,
Kawasha and his nation
Found out these holy rites."

It is worthy of note that on the same nuptial occasion the Tempest was acted by John Heming and the rest of the King's Company before Prince Charles, the Prince Palatine Elector and his bride, the Princess Elizabeth.

To such representations Crashaw appears to allude in the introduction to Whitaker's Good News from Virginia, when he speaks of the calumnies against the colony "and the jests of prophane players and other sycophants, and the flouts and mockes of some who by their age and profession should be no mockers."

The good clergyman, Samuel Purchas, wrote about the same time: "God Almighty prosper that the word may goe out of Bermuda, and the law of the Lord from Virginia, to a true conversion of the American world than hitherto our humorists, or Spanish insolence have intended."

In the Daily Prayer appointed for the Virginia Plantation, and published A. D. 1612, is this petition: "And, whereas, we have by undertaking this plantation undergone the reproofs of the base world, in so much as many of our own brethren laugh vs to scorne, O Lord, we pray Thee to fortifie vs against this temptation; let Sambullat and Tobias, Papist and *Players*, and such other Amonits and Horonits the scum and dregs of the earth, let them mocke such as help to build vp Jerusalem, and they that be filthy let them be filthy still."

The introductory epistle to a little book called "New Life of Virginia," also published A. D. 1612, asserts that "the malicious and looser sort, with the licentious vain stage poets, have whet their tongues with scornful taunt against the action itself, insomuch as there is no common reproach nor public name of any thing this day, except it be the name of God, which is more wildly defamed, traduced and derided by such unhallowed lips, than the name of Virginia."

In John Cook's play of "Tu Quoque, or The Cittie Gallant," published in London A. D. 1616, a penniless fellow says: "I dare not walk abroad to see my friends, for fear the sergeants should take acquaintance of me; my refuge is Ireland or Virginia."

John O. Halliwell, whose pains-taking research has thrown much light upon the writings of Shakspeare, discovered a poetical tract, "Newes from Virginia," published in A. D. 1610, in the library of the Earl of Charlemont, in Dublin, and knowing of no other copy in existence, in 1865, he had twenty-five copies printed, of which fifteen were destroyed, and ten were distributed.[1] As the earliest narrative which was published of the wreck of the Sea Venture, upon the Island of Devils, "otherwise called Bermoothawes," it is of interest to the students of the early English colonization of America. The writer, R. Rich, was one of those on board the Sea Venture, at the time of the wreck, and in a brief preface to the poem he calls himself a "soldier blunt and plain." In the list of the adventurers of the Virginia Company appear the names of Sir Robert Rich, who contributed seventy-five pounds, and one Robert Rich, who paid twelve pounds and ten shillings.

Sir Robert Rich, in A. D. 1617, sent out Capt. Thomas Jones, in the ship Lion to trade in the waters of India and Japan, and in 1619, Rich, now become the Earl of Warwick, hired Jones to go to Virginia, with a ship load of cattle, and after this, Jones, under a patent of the Virginia Company, sailed in the May Flower, with the Puritans who were landed on Plymouth Rock.

1 On August 16, 1611, John Wright, bookseller, entered at Stationers' Hall "A ballad. The last news fron Virginia, being an encouragement to all others to follow that noble enterprise." No copy of this ballad is known to have been preserved.

It may be that R. Rich, the writer of the poem, was a relative of Sir Robert Rich.

Shakspeare's latest composition is supposed to have been the play ot the Tempest, and was composed at the time when the Earl of Southampton, his friend, was disposed to talk much of the wreck of the Sea Venture, and the escape of its passengers, and was fitting out colonies to settle in Virginia, and Virginiola, as Bermudas was once called. It is not therefore surprising that we should find in the Tempest, allusions "to the vexed Bermoothes," the constant play of thunder and lightning, and a monster living on an isle of the sea.

The poem of Rich is of interest not only on account of its great rarity, but also of its being the first printed account of the wreck of the Sea Venture.

It was introduced to the reading public in a small quarto with the following title :

NEVVES FROM VIRGINIA.

THE LOST FLOCKE TRIUMPHANT;

With the happy Arrival of that famous and
worthy knight Sr Thomas Gates: and
the well reputed and valient Captaine Mr Christopher Newporte, and others, into
England.

With the manner of their distresse in the Iland of Devils
(otherwise called Bermoothawes) where they
remayned 42 weekes, and builded
two Pynaces, in which
they returned into
Virginia.

By R. RICH, GENT., one of the voyage.

LONDON:
Printed by Edw. Allde, and are to be solde by John
Wright, at Christ-Church dore. 1610.

TO THE READER.

READER,—how to stile thee I knowe not, perhaps learned, perhaps unlearned; happily captious, happily envious ; indeed, what or how to tearme thee I know not, only as I began I will proceede.

Reader : Thou dost peradventure imagine that I am mercenarie in this busines, and write for money (as your moderne Poets use) hyred by some of those ever to be admired adventurers to flatter the world. No ; I disclaime it. I have knowne the voyage, past the danger, seene that honorable work of Virginia, and I thanke God am arrivd here to tell thee what I have seene, don, and past. If thou wilt believe me, so ; if not, so to ; for I cannot force thee but to thy owne liking. I am a soldier, blunt and plaine, and so is the phrase of my newes ; and I protest it is true. If thou aske why I put it in verse, I prethee knowe it was onely to feede mine owne humour. I must confesse, that, had I not debarde myselfe of that large scope which to the writing of prose is allowed, I should have much easd myselfe, and given thee better content. But I intreat thee to take this as it is, and before many daies expire, I will promise thee the same worke more at large.

I did feare prevention by some of your writers, if they should have gotten but some part of the newes by the tayle, and therefore, though it be rude, let it passe with thy liking, and in so doing I shall like well of thee ; but, however, I have not long to stay. If thou wilt be unnaturall to thy countryman, thou maist, —I must not loose my patrymonie. I am for Virginia againe, and so I will bid the hartily farewell with an honest verse :

As I came hether to see my native land,
To waft me backe lend me thy gentle hand.

Thy loving Country-man,

R. R.

NEWES FROM VIRGINIA,

of the happy arrival of that famous and worthy knight, Sir Thomas Gates and well reputed and valiante Captaine Newport, into England.

" It is no idle fabulous tale,
  Nor is it fayned newes,
For *Truth* herself is heere arriv'd,
  Because you should not muse.
With her both Gates and Newport come,
  To tell *Report* doth lye,
Which did devulge into the world,
  That they at sea did dye.

'Tis true that eleaven monthes and more,
  These gallant worthy wights
Was in the shippe *Sea-Venture* nam'd,
  Deprived Virginia's sight :
And bravely did they glyde the maine,
  Till Neptune 'gan to frowne,
As if a courser proudly backt
  Would throwe his ryder downe.

The seas did rage, the windes did blowe,
  Distressed were they then ;
Their shippe did leake, her tacklings breake,
  In daunger were her men,
But heaven was pylotte in this storme,
  And to an iland nere,
Bermoothawes called, conducted them,
  Which did abute their feare.

But yet these worthies forced were,
 Opprest with weather againe,
To runne their ship between two rockes,
 Where she doth still remaine ;
And then on shoare the iland came,
 Inhabited by hogges,
Some foule, and tortoyses there were,
 They onley had one dogge.

To kill these swyne to yield them foode
 That little had to eate,
Their store was spent, and all things scant,
 Alas ! they wanted meate.
A thousand hogges that dogge did kill,
 Their hunger to sustaine,
And with such foode, did in that ile
 Two and forty weekes remaine,

And there two gallant pynases
 Did build of seader-tree
The brave *Deliverance* one was call'd
 Of seaventy tonne was shee,
The other, *Patience* had to name,
 Her burthen thirty tonne ;
Two only of their men which there,
 Pale death did overcome.

And for the losse of these two soules,
 Which were accounted deere,
A sonne and daughter then was borne,
 And were baptized there.
The two and forty weekes being past,
 They hoyst sayle and away ;
Their ships with hogs well freighted were,
 Their harts with mickle joy.

And so to Virginia came,
 Where these brave soldiers finde
The English-men opprest with griefs
 And discontent in minde ;
They seem'd distracted and forlorne
 For those two worthies' losse,
Yet at their home returne, they joye'd,
 Amongst them some were crosse.

And in the midst of discontent
  Came noble Delaware ;
And heard the griefes on either part,
  And sett them free from care :
He comforts them, and cheeres their hearts,
  That they abound with joy ;
He feedes them full, and feedes their soules,
  With God's word every day.

A discreet counsell he creates
  Of men of worthy fame,
That noble Gates, leiftenant was,
  The admiral had to name ;
The worthy Sir George Somers, knight,
  And others of command ;
Maister George Pearcy, which is brother
  Unto Northumberland.

Sir Fardinando Wayneman, knight,
  And others of good fame,
That noble lord his company
  Which to Virginia came,
And landed there, his number was
  One hundred seaventy ; then
Ad to the rest, and they make full
  Foure hundred able men.

Where they unto their labour fall,
  As men that mean to thrive ;
Let's pray that heaven may blesse them all
  And keep them long alive :
Those men that vagrants liv'd with us,
  Have there deserved well,
Their governour writes in their praise
  As divers letters tel.

And to the adventurers thus he writes,
  Be not dismayed at all,
For scandall cannot doe us wrong,
  God will not let us fall.
Let England knowe our willingnesse,
  For that our worke is good,
Wee hope to plant a nation,
  Where none before hath stood.

To glorifie the Lord 'tis done,
And to no other end;
He that would crosse so good a worke,
To God can be no friend;
There is no feare of hunger here
For corne much store here growes,
Much fish the gallant rivers yield,
'Tis truth, without suppose.

Great store of fowle, of venison,
Of grapes and mulberries,
Of chesnuts, walnuts and such like
Of fruits and strawberries,
There is indeed no want at all
But some, condicion'd ill,
That wish the worke should not goe on,
With words doe seeme to kill.

And for an instance of their store,
The noble Delaware
Hath for a present hither sent,
To testifie his care
In managing so good a worke,
Two gallant ships, by name
The *Blessing* and the *Hercules*
Well fraught, and in the same

Two ships, are these commodities
Furres, sturgeon, caviare,
Black walnut-tree, and some deale boards,
With such they laden are;
Some pearle, some wainscot and clapbords.
With some sasafras wood,
And iron promis't for 'tis true
Their mynes are very good.

Then maugre, scandall, false report
Or any opposition,
Th' adventurers doe thus devulge
To men of good condition,
That he that wants shall have reliefe
Be he of honest minde,
Apparel, coyne, or anything,
To such they will be kinde,

To such as to Virginia
  Do purpose to repaire;
And when that they shall hither come,
  Each man shall have his share,
Day wages for the laborer,
  And for his more content,
A house and garden plot shall have,
  Besides 'tis further ment

That every man shall have a part,
  And not thereof denied
Of generall profit, as if that he
  Twelve pounds, ten shillings paid;
And he that in Virginia
  Shall copper coyne receive,
For hyer, or commodities,
  And will the country leave

Upon delivery of such coyne
  Unto the Governour,
Shall by exchange, at his returne,
  Be by their treasurer
Paid him in London, at first sight,
  No man shall cause to grieve
For 'tis their general will and wish
  That every man shall live.

The number of adventurers,
  That are for this plantation,
Are full eight hundred worthy men,
  Some noble, all of fashion;
Good, discreete, their work is good,
  May heaven assist them in their worke,
And thus our newes is done."

Gates, Newport, and Rich found Virginia, everywhere, evil spoken of, upon their arrival in September, 1610, in London.

The seven ships from which they had been separated in the storm, had safely arrived in the summer of 1609, at Jamestown. The passengers were an "unhallowed crew." Twenty-eight or thirty were sent in the ship Swallow to trade for corn with the Indians, and never returned. Those who reached England told horrible tales, the recital of which caused the hair of the flesh to stand up. They asserted that the colonists were starving and feeding upon rats, mice, snakes and toad-stools; that an Indian had been dug out of his grave and eaten; and that one man killed his wife as she slept upon his bosom, cut her in pieces, powdered her, and fed upon her, till he had eaten all of her body except the head. Sir Thomas Gates found that this story met him everywhere, and he softened it somewhat by stating that the man hated his wife and killed and cut her in pieces, and as an excuse plead hunger, but he was tried, found guilty, and burned to death.

It was necessary by "Newes from Virginia," and other pamphlets, to reassure the London merchants, who had become despondent, and bravely assert—

"For scandal cannot do us wrong,
God will not let us fall,
Let England know our willingness
For that our work is good,
We hope to plant a nation
Where none before hath stood."

Shakspeare died, A.D. 1616, before his patron, the Earl of Southampton, became the presiding officer of the Virginia Company of London. The great dramatist loved to stop at the Crown Inn, Oxford, and was godfather to a son of the handsome landlady. The godson became a poet, and early in 1650, as Sir William Davenant, was commissioned by Charles the Second as Governor of that part of Virginia, known as Maryland. On his voyage he was captured by one of the ships of Parliament, brought back to England and lodged in the Tower, where he finished his poem of Gondibert, and was at length set free by the friendly intercession of the great Puritan, John Milton.

DOCUMENTS

FOR THE FIRST TIME PRINTED,

ILLUSTRATIVE OF THE

ENGLISH COLONIZATION OF AMERICA.

The following correspondence copied by the courtesy of the Mayor of Sandwich, from the ancient archives of that town, will be read with interest by all students of Virginia history and the English Colonization of America.

Sir Edwin Sandys was knighted by King James in 1603, the same year that the philosopher Francis Bacon received the honor. The second son of the Archbishop of York, he attended one of the colleges of Oxford in 1577 when about sixteen years of age. In early manhood he traveled on the continent and wrote "Europæ Speculum, or The State of Religion in the Western Parts of the World," and was several times a member of the House of Commons.

With the celebrated Lord Bacon he prepared, in 1604, a remonstrance against the title of the King of Great Britain being assumed by James, in which were set forth the now accepted principles of popular liberty. For services rendered the government he received an estate at Norburne, or Northburne, six miles in the country, from the port of Sandwich, and here he established his residence. For years he was an active promoter of the colonization of America, and on the 26th of April, 1619 was elected the presiding officer of the Virginia Company of London, in place of Sir Thomas Smith. The town of Sandwich in 1620 chose him, after a "tumultuous election," as their representative in Parliament, and during the recess, by order of the King, he was placed under arrest, with the Lords

Oxford, Southampton, and other opponents of arbitrary rule. When the House of Commons assembled again in November, 1621, the members were indignant at the confinement of Sandys. Sir George Calvert, the King's secretary, also a member, afterwards the projector of the province of Maryland, with acrimony told James the First the feelings of Parliament, and he wrote an angry letter complaining of the "fiery, popular and turbulent spirits" of the House, and denying their right of petition in points he had forbidden to be discussed. Pym and other members of a committee, carried to the King a reply, and he again answered in arrogant sentences. Hallam states that the court now became alarmed, and sent Calvert to the House of Commons with an explanatory message, but the storm could not be allayed by calling the King's language "a slip of the pen, at the close of a long letter." The House, to the last, firmly asserted that there should be freedom of debate, and "from all impeachment, imprisonment and molestation" for anything said on the floor of Parliament.

While Sandys was under arrest officers were sent to search his house. His high-toned wife, with womanly dignity, bore the inquisition of her drawers and jewelry casket, but when the key to her husband's papers was demanded, an indignant heart forced this utterance from her lips, "I wish his majesty had a key to unlock her husband's heart, that he might see that not anything was there but loyalty."

A few months after Sandys became the head of the Virginia Company, on the 9th of June, 1619, O. S., a patent was granted largely by his influence to John Whincop[1] for the use of the Puritans at Leyden, which was never used, but on the 2d of the next February at a meeting held in his house near Aldersgate, a patent was granted to John Peirce and associates, under which the May Flower sailed and landed its passengers at Plymouth Rock.

On the 9th of June, 1620, Sandys wrote from his country seat at Northburne to Buckingham, that he would cheerfully serve one

1 In the London Company's transactions of May 26, 1619, Whincop is spoken of as: "One Mr. Whincop commended to the company by the Earl of Lincoln, intending in person to go to Virginia." On Easter Sunday A. D. 1632, three brothers, John, Samuel and Thomas Whincop, preached in the church of St. Mary's Spittle, London. In A. D. 1642, the chaplain of the Puritan Lord Say was a Rev. Dr. Whincop, Rector of St. Martin's in the field, London.

year more as the head of the Virginia Company, but the King was opposed, and said to some of the members that Sandys was his greatest enemy, and that he could hardly think well of any one who was his friend, and working himself into a passion exclaimed, "Choose the devil if you will, but not Sir Edwin Sandys." In view of this opposition the Company, on the 19th of June elected the Earl of Southampton as his successor.

Sandys lived until he was nearly seventy years of age, died in October, 1629, and was buried at Northburne. In his will he left a legacy of £1,500 to establish a lecture on metaphysics at Oxford. He was married four times. One of his sons, Edwin, a colonel under Cromwell, fell in battle on the 3d of September, 1651, at Worcester.[1]

The first of his letters on file in the archives of Sandwich was written at Northborne on the 21st of March, A. D. 1610, Old Style, but A. D. 1611, according to modern computation, and addressed to the Mayor and Jurats of that port.

---

1 In October, 1621, George, the brother of Sir Edwin Sandys, arrived at Jamestown as Treasurer of Virginia. His father, Archbishop Sandys, made this entry in the family Bible: "George Sandes, born the seventh day of March, at six of the clock in the morning, 1577. His god-fathers, George, Earl of Cumberland and William, Lord Ewer. His god-mother, Catharine, Countess of Huntington."

Before he left England he had published a translation of five books of Ovid, to which the poet Drayton alluded in a rhyming letter sent to Virginia:

"And worthy George, by industry and use,
Let's see what lines Virginia will produce;
Go on with Ovid, as you have begun
With the first five books; let your numbers run
Glib as the former, so shall it live long,
And do much honour to the English tongue,
Entice the Muses, thither to repair,
Entreat them gently, train them to that air,
* * * * * * *
But you may save your labour, if you please,
To write to me aught of your savages,
As savage slaves, be in Great Britain here,
As you can show me there."

While at Jamestown "worthy George" translated the remaining books of Ovid, and in 1626, after he returned to England, the whole was published at London, in an elegant illustrated folio. Fuller, the historian, wrote, "Master Sandys was altogether as dexterous at inventing as translating, and his own poems as spriteful, vigorous and masculine. He lived to be a very aged man whom I saw in the Savoy, in 1641, having a youthful soul in a decayed body."

He resided at the house of his niece, the widow of Francis Wyatt, Governor of Virginia. In the Register of Bexley Abbey, Kent, is this entry: "Georgius Sandys, Poetarum Anglorum sui sœculi facile princeps. sepultus fuit Martii 7 stilo Anglico. An. Dom. 1643."

Sr.

I am requested by his Maties Counsil for Virginia to conveigh these inclosed, to yor hands & to procure yor answer against the beginning of the next term. The effect is to inuite yor town & such particular persons of worth as shall be so disposed, to partnership in the great action of Virginia, w'ch after manifold disasters doth now, under the government of noble & worthie leaders, begin to revive, and we trust ere long shall flourish.

I acquainted them that yor Town had been much hindered by sickness: in regard whereof the lesse will be perhaps expected. But they would not pass over so principal a port, in an action tending generally to the good of the whole Realm, but the profit whereof will chiefly fall to the Hauen Towns, & principally in them, to merchants.

But I will leave you to the letter itself; only thus much (to acquaint yu wth the present state of the busines): we have sent away Sr Thomas Dale wth 300 men & great abundance of victual & furniture. We send after them, this next month two ships more wth 100 Kyne & 200 swine for breed.[1] And if monie come in, whereof we are in very good hope, in May next we shall send Sr Thomas Gates wth other 300 men of the best and choicest we

1 Sir Thomas Dale before reaching manhood entered the army of the Netherlands, and rose to a position of honor. Winwood, the English Ambassador to that country, in March, A. D. 1604, was informed by the Secretary of State, that King James wished him to "take notice of his gracious opinion of the merit of Captain Dale, both for having been a valiant and long servitor, and having for the most part" served at his own charges.

In June, 1606, the King of England knighted him as Sir Thomas Dale of Surrey. Retaining his commission in the army of the Netherlands, he left the Thames with a party of colonists in February, and reached Jamestown on the 12th of May, A. D. 1610. With John Rolfe. Pocahontas and a party of Indians he returned to England in June, 1616. His wife was Elizabeth, daughter of Sir Thomas Throckmorton, Kt, and sister of Sir William Throckmorton, Baronet. Toward the close of the year 1617, he was made commander of the fleet of the East India Company. In February, 1618, after making his will and provision for his wife, he embarked for the Indian Ocean. On the voyage from Engano in the Malay Archipelago, to Masulipatam he became sick and on the 19th of July, 1619, soon after his arrival at the latter place, died.

He left no children. His wife's will, made on 4th of July, and proved on 2d of December, 1640, directed that her debts should be paid out of the estate in the hands of the East India Company and her estate in Virginia. The statement that Sir Thomas Dale had been twice married appears to be incorrect.

can procure.[1] W'ch done, and God blessing them, the busines we account is wonn.

Thus wth my very heartie salutations, I betake y^{u} to the Tuition & Direction of the Highest, & rest,

Y^{r} very loving friend,

EDWIN SANDYS.

Norborn,

21 Martii, 1610.

The letter forwarded from the Virginia Company by Sandys was sent from Sir Thomas Smith's house, in Philpot Lane, London, where the meetings of the corporation were then held, and is as follows:

LETTER OF VIRGINIA COMPANY.

"The eyes of all Europe looking upon our endevours to spread the Gospell among the Heathen people of Virginia, to plant o^{r} English nation there, & to settle at in those p'ts wch maie be peculiar to o^{r} nation, so that we may thereby be secured from being eaten out of all proffits of trade, by our more industrious neighbors, wee cannot doubt but that the eyes of also of y^{or} best judgments and affections are fixed no lesse upon a designe of soe great consequence.

The reasons that action hath not yet received the successe of o^{r} desires and and expectac'ons are published in print to all the world, To repeat them all were idlenes in us & must bee tedious to you, yet to omytt mention of that mayne reason w'ch hath shaken the whole frame of this business & w'ch hath begott theise o^{r} requests to you, would but returne unto us a fruitlesse accompt and consequentlie a hazard to destroie that life w'ch yet breatheth in this action.

1 Sir Thomas Gates, while in the military service of the Netherlands, obtained leave of absence to go with the expedition to Virginia. In the summer of the year 1610, he was sent back to England by Lord Delaware to procure supplies and represent the interest of the Colony. In June, 1611, he sailed again for Virginia in charge of a number of immigrants, and accompanied by his wife and daughters. His wife died at sea, and in August he reached Jamestown. In December his daughters returned to England with Captain Newport. In the spring of 1614 Gates left Virginia and never returned. It has been said that he died in the service of the East India Company. Sir Dudley Digges, while sojourning at Amsterdam, in 1621, in a letter to the English Ambassador at the Hague, sends his "love to the honest Sir Tho's Gates."

That reason in few wordes was want of meanes to imploie good men, & want of just payment of the meanes which weare promised, so disabling us therebie to set forth or supplies in due season.

Now that we have established a form of gonrment fitt for such members in the p'sons of the Lord La Warr and Sr George Sommers allready in those p'ts, as also in Sr Thomas Dale embarqt w'th 300 men & provisions for them, and the Collony to the value of many thousands of pounds, who is already falne downe the ryver, in his waie thither, & in Sr Thomas Gates whom we reserve to second this expedicon, in Maie next, with 300 more of the choicest p'sons wee can gett for moneys through your means & our own cares.

Wee accompt from many advised consultacons that 30,000£ to bee paid in two years, for three supplies, will be a sufficient sum to settle there, a very able and strong foundacon of anexing another kingdome to this Crowne.[1]

Of this 30,000£ there is allready signed by diverse p'ticular noblemen, gentn and merchants the some of 18,000 as maie appeare unto you by a true copy of their names and somes, written with their own hands in a Register booke w'ch remaynes as a recorde in the hands of Sr Thomas Smith. Threr, for that plantacon, so that the adventures to be procured from all the noblemen, the Byshopps & Clergie that have not yet signed from all the Gentrie, Merchants and Corporate townes of this Kingdome, doth but amount to 12,000£ payable as aforesaid.

To accomplish w'ch sum wee entreate yor favours no farther than amongst yorselves, and as shall seeme good unto you upon respect of your judgments, ranck and place: we endevour by theis or requests to gaine as helpes unto vs, in such poor measure as wee have begun toward the advancement of soe gloryous an action.

Wee are farther to entreate yor helpes to procure vs such nombers of men & of such condicon as you are willing and able; wee send you herewth the list of the nombers & qualitie that we entende, God willing, to employ in Maie next.

1 In 1619 the Virginia Company adopted as a motto of its Seal: "En! dat Virginia quintam." Behold! Virginia gives a fifth crown.

As soon as you can wth conveniency wee desire yor resolucons touching meanes and men, upon receipt thereof wee shall acknowledge due thanks & lymitt the time of their appearance, wherein wee shall not forgett the pointe of charge to the undertakers, howsoever we preferre so farre as lyes in us, a seasonable dispatch to the first place of o^r consideracons.

The benefitt by this action, if it shall please God to blesse these begynnings wth a happye successe must arise to the generall good of this Common wealth. To laie then a stronge foundacon of soe great a work wee hold o^rselves & o^r request to yo^rs, warranted by the reasons aforesaid & by the rules of honour & judgment, & for as wee o^rselves, the p'sent adventurers cannott receive the whole benefitt, soe can it not be expected that we should undergoe the whole charge. The often renewed complaints against Companyes heretofore hath happened by reason of the Monopolizings of trade into a few men's hands, and though the ice of this busnes hath been broken by the purses, cares, and adventures of a few, yet wee seclude no subject from the future benefitt of o^r present care, charge and hazard of p'son & adventures, all w'ch we leave to yor judicious consideracons & only importune yor speedy resolucons, that according to the warrants of duty wee maie either wash o^r hands from further care or cheerfully embrace strength from you to the furtherance of this action, that tends so directly to advance the glory of God, the honor of o^r English nation & the profitt and securitie in o^r judgment, of this Kingdome,

And soe leaving you to that sence hereof w'ch his goodness shall please to infuse into you, who is of absolute power to dispose of all things to the best, wee rest.

Yo^r very loving friends,

From Sr Thomas Smyths' house in Philpot Lane, the 28th of February, 1610.

PEMBROKE,[1]
MONTGOMERY,
SOUTHAMPTON,[3]
LISLE,[4]

[Sir] WALTER COPE,
" G. COPPIN,
" [Illegible,]
" THO. SMYTHE,
" H. FANSHAW.

[Sir] THOMAS GATES,
" ROBERT MANSELL,
" EDWIN SANDYS,
" BAPTIST HICKS,

1 William, Earl of Pembroke.
2 Philip, " Montgomery.
3 Henry, " Southampton.
4 Robert, Lord Lisle, afterwards Lord of Leicester.

Boys, in "Collections for the history of Sandwich," states that the town in 1609 granted £25 as a venture for the settlement of Virginia, and it is without doubt in reference to this that the following letter was addressed on the 8th of April, 1612—

"*To the Right Wo^thie^, my very loving friends, the Mayor and Jurates of Sandwich :*

GENTLEMEN—I am required by his Maties counsel for Virginia, to call on you for the twenty-five pounds wch long since y^u^ promised to adventure wth them, towards the furthering of that plantation. And have received from them a Bill of adventure under their seale to be delivered unto you upon paiment of that sum, wch Bill I have sent you by Mr Parke to be disposed accordingly.

I am also in their names very earnestly to pray y^or^ furtherance, towards the furthering of a Lotterie lately granted to them by his Matie. The use and nature thereof y^u^ shall perceive by the proclamation concerning it, which I have also sent. And Mr Mayor of Sandwich is particularly desired to receive & return such monies as men shall be disposed to adventure in it, according to such instructions as are contained in a book sent to you for that purpose : presuming greatly of your affectionate rediness to aid & advance so worthie an enterprise tending so greatly to the enlargement of the Cristian truth, the honor of o^r^ nation, and benefit of English people, as by God's assistance the sequell in short time will manifest. The example also hereof, now benficiall in y^or^ best & most needful occasions, it may prove unto y^or^selfs I know in your wisdome y^u^ will easily see and consider. So with my very hartie salutations I commend y^u^ to the divine tuition and rest.

Y^r^ very loving friend,

NORTHBORN, EDWIN SANDYS.

8 Aprile, 1612.

Less than a month after Gates arrived, Lord Delaware landed, on the 10th of June, 1610, at Jamestown, but on March 28th, 1611, he visited England on account of ill health, leaving George Percy Deputy Governor. At that time, the only other place inhabited by whites, was Point Comfort, which consisted of a small fort fenced with palisadoes, one dwelling, a store, and a few thatched cabins.

After the name of Robert Hunt, preacher, in the list of the members of the expedition who settled at Jamestown in 1607, is that of George Percy. An honorable man, the descendant of an honorable house, uncomplaining under peculiar hardships, and faithful to his trust, it is to be regretted that so so few incidents of his life have been preserved.

He was the brother of the Duke of Northumberland, and his narrative of the plantation of the southern colony in Virginia, ending at September, 1607, abridged and published by Purchas, is full of interest.

With Gabriel Archer and John Smith he accompanied Captain Newport in the first explorations of the James river in the vicinity of Richmond, After Captain Smith's term as President of the Council expired, the colonists, in the absence of Sir Thomas Gates, who had been wrecked at Bermudas, chose Percy as president.

A dispatch to the Earl of Salisbury, Secretary of State under King James, dated October 4, 1609, written by one of the senior captains of the vessels of the Gates and Somers expedition, states that "they found all the Council dead but Captain Smith, who reigned sole Governor, and is now sent home to answer some misdemeanors. George Percy, brother to my Lord Northumberland, is elected President, and Mr. West, brother to Lord Delaware, of the Council, with Captain Martin."

Among the papers in the library of the present Earl of Northumberland there is evidence that there was an affectionate interest felt by the Northumberland family in their representative in Virginia. Amid many entries in an expense-book, kept in the days of James the First, the following are found: A charge of £9, 2s., 6d. for clothing sent to Mr. George Percy by Captain Newport; and also a payment of 14 shillings to Mr. Melshawe for many necessaries which he delivered to Mr. Percy toward the building of a house in Virginia. On February the 6th, 1610, payments to the amount of £432, 1s., 6d. were made by the head of the Northumberland family for Mr. Percy. There appears also a payment by the Duke of Northumberland in 1607–'8 of 3 shillings for rings and other pieces of copper given to the Virginia Prince; of 8 shillings for cutting a large and small Virginia stone; 24 shillings for gold, and 15 shillings for setting the large Virginia stone in gold. In 1610 a Declaration of the State of Virginia was printed, and a copy was purchased for 6 shillings for the Northumberland family.

Upon the arrival of Sir Thomas Gates in May, 1610, from the Bermudas, Percy ceased to act as President, and Gates became the Governor under the new charter until the coming of Lord Delaware, two weeks later. Delaware, as Governor-General, made Percy one of the Council. In March, 1611, Delaware, on account of ill-health, sailed from Jamestown, and Gates, the Lieutenant Governor, being in England, Percy was appointed Deputy-Governor. Among the Northumberland papers there is the following letter, written to his brother Henry, and dated August 17, 1611, which probably was brought to England in the ship Star, which arrived there about the 1st of December with Captain Newport.

Right Hono^{ble}:

I am not ignorant, and cannot be therefore unmindfull in what I may so satisfie your Lo^{p} for your manifold and continuall curtesies wch I dayly and at the reprotch of everie shipping do abundantly taste of, and I must acknowledg freely that this last yere hath not bin a little chardgable unto your Honnor who I hope will continue so noble and hono^{ble} opinion of me as you shall not think any thing prodigally by me wasted or spent wch tendeth to my no little advancement: True it is the place wch I hold in this Colonie, (the store affording no other meanes then a pound of meale) cannot be de defraied wth small expense, it standing upon my reputation (being Governeur of James Towne) to keepe a continuall and dayly Table for Gentlemen of fashion aboute me, my request unto y^{r} Lo^{p}. at this present is to intreate your Honnor to be highly pleased to dischardg a Bill of my hand made to Mr Nellson, and likewise a Bill of eight pounds unto Mr Pindle Burie of Lond^{o} merchant and I shall ever be in all humble dutie bound unto your Lo^{p}: And thus wishing all honnor and happines to accompanie you in this world and eternall blisse in the other to come I cease to be further vnnecessary troublesome vnto your Lop. ever vowing my self and the vttmost of my services in all duty unto your Honno[r]. and rest.

Your Lordship's
louinge brother

VIRGINIA, James
Towne, August 17, 1611.

GEORGE PERCY.

[Addressed:] To the right Hono[ble] my singuler good
Lord and Brother, The Earle of
Northumberland, give these.

The Secretary of the Virginia Historical Society, R. A. Brock, Esq., states that there is among the collections of that Society a fine portrait of Captain George Percy, which, together with one of Lord Culpepper, was donated to the Society by Charles Wykeham Martin, Esq., of Leeds Castle, England, in 1853. The frames accommodating each of these portraits are of solid British oak, handsomely carved and gilded, and were presented with them by William Twopenny, Esq., of London.

ERRATA.

Page 9. "John" should read "George" Kendall.
Page 13. "Narative" should read "narrative."
Page 20. "Surving" should read "surviving."

NOTES

ON THE

VIRGINIA COLONIAL CLERGY.

BY

EDWARD D. NEILL,

PRESBYTER OF REFORMED EPISCOPAL CHURCH.

REPRINTED FROM EPISCOPAL RECORDER.

PHILADELPHIA:
1220 SANSOM STREET.
1877.

Extract from Sermon of Patrick Copland, before the Virginia Company, preached at Bow Church, London, Thursday, April 18, 1622.

"And, that I may bend my speech unto all, seeing so many of the Lord's worthies have done worthily in this noble action; yea, and seeing that some of them greatly rejoice in this, that God hath enabled them to help forward this glorious work, both with their prayers and with their purses, let it be your grief and sorrow to be exempted from the company of so many honorable-minded men, and from this noble plantation, tending so highly to the advancement of the Gospel, and to the honoring of our dread Sovereign, by enlarging of his kingdoms, and adding a fifth crown unto his other four: for '*En dat Virginia quintam*' is the motto of the legal seal of Virginia."

VIRGINIA COLONIAL CLERGY.

CHAPTER I.

CHAPLAINS OF EARLY EXPEDITIONS.

Edward Maria Wingfield, the President of the First Council of Virginia, makes the following statement, relative to the first clergyman who arrived, in 1607, with the founders of Jamestown:—

REV. ROBERT HUNT.

"For my first worke, which was to make right choice of a spiritual pastor, I appeeled to the remembrance of my Lo. of Caunt., his Grace, who gave me very gracious audience in my request. And the world knoweth when I took with me truly a man, in my opinion, not any waie to be touched with the rebellious humor of a papist spirit, nor blemished with the least suspicion of a factious schismatic."

The appointment of Robert Hunt as chaplain of Newport's expedition to Virginia came through the direct agency of Richard Hakluyt, Prebend of Westminster, who was an earnest advocate for the planting of an English colony in America.

Anderson supposes that he had been a rector in Kent, before he received the position of chaplain. Amid all the dissensions of the first colonists, he proved himself a gentle shepherd, and won the respect of all classes. President Wingfield speaks of him as follows: "Two or three Sunday mornings the Indians gave us alarms; by that times they were answered, the place about us well discovered, and our divine service ended, the day was far spent. The preacher did ask me if it were my pleasure to have a sermon; he said he was prepared for it. I made answer, that our men were weary and hungry, and that he did see the time of the day far spent (for at other times he never made such question, but the service finished, he began his sermon), and that if it pleased him, we would spare him till some other time. I never failed to take such notes, by writing, out of his doctrine as my capacity would comprehend, unless some rainy day hindered my endeavors."

On rainy days the place of worship was not very comfortable. The congregation assembled in fair weather under an old sail, suspended from trees, but when it rained service was held in a rotten tent. In time the colonists constructed a barn-like edifice, with a roof of turf and earth resting upon rafters, and in this place, as humble as the manger of Bethlehem, Hunt officiated as long as he lived.

In the winter of 1609 a fire broke out, which destroyed Hunt's library, and before the summer of 1609 he had died, but the precise time has not been ascertained.

REV. MR. GLOVER.

In June, A. D. 1611, Sir Thomas Gates left England on a second voyage to Virginia. William Crashaw, the celebrated divine, father of the poet, says that the Rev. Mr. Glover accompanied him, who had been "an approved preacher in Bedford and Huntingdonshire, a graduate of Cambridge, reverenced and respected," but he soon died.

Crashaw writes, "He endured not the sea-sickness of the countrey so well as younger and stronger bodies; and so, after zealous and faithful performance of his ministeriall dutie, whilest he was able, he gave his soule to Christ Jesus (under whose banner he went to fight, and for whose glorious name's sake, he undertook the danger) more worthy to be accounted a true confessor of Christ than hundreds that are canonized in the Pope's Marytyrologie."

ALEXANDER WHITAKER, MINISTER AT HENRICO, VIRGINIA, A. D. 1611–1617.

Crashaw, the father of the poet, and a distinguished divine, in the year 1613, alludes to the ministers who had gone to America as able and fit men, "all of them graduates, allowed preachers, single men, having no pastoral cares, nor charge of children," and exhorts them in these words: "Though Satan visibly and palpably reigns there, more than in any other known place in the world, yet be of courage, blessed brethren; God will tread Satan under your feet shortly, and the ages to come will eternize your names, as the apostles of Virginia." Among these so-called apostles, one who came with Sir Thomas Dale, in 1611, was Alexander Whitaker. He had been comfortably settled in the north of England for five or six years, after graduating at Cambridge, when he tore himself away from comforts and friends, and "his warm nest," constrained by the love of Christ to become a missionary. He was the son of the great scholar, William Whitaker, for many years Professor of Divinity, and Master of St. John's College, Cambridge, of whom a poet said: "He was the shield of truth, the scourge of error." With his father he held the then prevailing opinions of the Church of England. He taught that a bishop and presbyter in the New Testament were of the same order, and that the only Apostolical Succession was based upon the presentation of Scriptural truths. "If," said the elder Whitaker, "he is a perfect minister who has learned the scriptural doctrine, and explained it to the people, then that is a true and perfect Church which receives and cherishes such doctrine."

The son had been taught, also, that baptism purifies none, except those who receive the promise of gratuitous justification in Christ, and that there was nothing like a real, express presence in the elements upon the Lord's Table.

But one of Alexander Whitaker's sermons was published. In 1613 it was printed in London, and contains the following sentence:—

"Let not the servants of superstition, that think to merit by their good works, go beyond us in well-doing, neither let them be able to open their mouths against us, and to condemn the religion of our Protestation, for want of charitable deeds."

Sir Thomas Dale had passed many years among the Presbyterians of Holland, before coming to Virginia. His first wife was a relative, and his second wife a sister of Sir W. Throckmorton, a man of Puritan affinities. Many of the settlers at Henrico were Dutchmen, and it was to be expected that Whitaker's views would be in sympathy with Low-Churchmen, the prevailing party among the people of England.

Hamor, the secretary of the Colony, in a narrative published in London, in 1615, prints a letter of Whitaker's, written in June, 1614, which contains the earliest account of a church organization among the English of North America. He writes: "Every Sabbath day we preach in the forenoon, and catechize in the afternoon. Every Saturday, at night, I exercise in Sir Thomas Dale's house. Our Church affairs be consulted on by the Minister and four of the most religious men. Once every month we have a communion, and once a year a solemn fast."

The weekly religious service, or exercise, on Saturday night, was a characteristic of the Puritans within the Church of England. Purchas states that the surplice was not even spoken of in Whitaker's parish. The consultation with four of the most religious men resembled a Dutch consistory.

Before June, 1617, Whitaker was drowned, and William Wickham, a pious man, without Episcopal ordination, conducted the services at Henrico. In 1621 Rev. Jonas Stockton took charge of the parish.

The unreliable John Smith published a letter, purporting to have been written by the Rev. Jonas Stockham, on May 20th, 1621, which Purchas states was addressed to Alexander Whitaker. Alluding to the Indians, he remarks: "We have sent boys among them to learn their language, but they return worse than they went; but I am no statesman, nor love I to meddle with anything but my books, but I can find no probability by this course to draw them to goodness; and I am persuaded if Mars and Minerva go hand-in-hand, they will effect more good in one hour, than these verbal Mercurians in their lives. And till their Priests and Ancients have their throats cut, there is no hope to bring them to conversion."

This sentiment, attributed to Stockham, we find in almost similar language in a letter written on April 15th, 1609, by the historiographer, Richard Hakluyt, to the Virginia Company. His words relative to the Indians are, "They be also as unconstant as the weathercock, and most ready to take all occasions to do mischief. They are great liars and dissemblers, for which faults oftentimes they had their deserved payments. And many times they gave good testimonies of their great valor and resolution. To handle them gently, while gentle courses may be found to serve, it will be without comparison the best; but if gentle polishing will not serve, the one shall not want hammerers and rough masons enow—I mean our old soldiers trained up in the Netherlands—to square and prepare them to our preachers' hands."

No such letter could have been written to Whitaker, as alleged, in 1621, for in 1617 he was drowned. There was no Rev. Jonas Stockham in Virginia, but in 1620 there arrived, in the "Bona Nova," the Rev. Jonas Stockton, about thirty-six years of age, with a son Timothy, ten years old, and for a time he was minister at Henrico and New Bermudas.

At the instance of Sir William Throckmorton, in 1620, one of the Indian girls brought to London by Sir Thomas Dale in 1616, being weak with consumption, was sent to the house of a cousin of Whitaker, the Rev. William Gouge, who "took great pains to comfort her, both in soul and body." Gouge was a Cambridge graduate, noted for scholarship, oratory, piety and philanthropy. He was a member of the Westminster Assembly of Divines, and died in December, 1653, after a pastorate of forty-five years at Black Friars, London.

CHAPTER II.

CLERGY FROM A.D. 1619 TO A.D. 1630.

Hunt, Glover, and Whitaker had all been summoned to the "better land" before the assembling at Jamestown, on July 30th, 1619, of the first American legislature.

RICHARD BUCK, CHAPLAIN OF THE "SEA VENTURE."

Richard Buck, who had been an Oxford student, was "an able and painful preacher," commended to honest Sir Thomas Gates by Bishop Ravis, of London, one of the translators of the King James' version of the Bible, a prelate of mildness and liberality.

He embarked in 1609, in the "Sea Venture," with Gates, Somers, and Captain Newport, and during a violent storm in the last days of July, the ship was wrecked at Bermudas. Here the passengers and sailors remained several months, and Buck was faithful in the discharge of his duties.

Strachey, Secretary of Virginia, says:—During our time of abode upon these islands, we had every Sunday two sermons preached by our minister, besides every morning and evening, at the ringing of a bell, we repaired all to public prayer, at what time the names of our whole company were called, and such as were wanting were duly punished." He was occupied while there in baptizing, burying, and marrying.

John Rolfe, whose name has become distinguished as the first man who established a tobacco plantation in Virginia, and linked with the romance about Pocahontas, was, with his white wife, passenger on the "Sea Venture." Mrs. Rolfe gave birth to a daughter, and on the 4th of February, 1609–10, she was christened Bermuda; Strachey and Captain Newport standing as "witnesses.". After a brief existence the child was buried on the Island.

A ship of seventy tons, named the "Deliverance," having been built, in it, and a small pinnace, called the "Patience," the party left, and in the latter part of May, 1610, arrived at Jamestown. Sir Thomas Gates, before he unrolled his commission and commenced his duties as Governor, caused the bell to be rung, and then the emaciated and desponding colonists listened to the "zealous and sorrowful prayer of Mr. Buck." On Sunday, the 10th of June, Lord Delaware arrived as Governor General, and immediately went ashore and heard "a sermon made by Mr. Buck." The church in which this sermon was preached a chronicle of that day described as "a homely thing, like a barn set upon crutchets, covered with rafts, sedge and earth; so was also the walls."

Lord Delaware ordered the church to be repaired, and when completed it was twenty-four by sixty feet in dimensions, the pews made of cedar, the communion table of black walnut, a baptismal font hollowed out of a log like a canoe, and two bells on the west gable.

Every Sunday two sermons were delivered by Buck, or Glover, or Whitaker; and the Puritan custom of a sermon or lecture on Thursday was also observed. During the services, if present, Lord Delaware sat in the chancel, in a green velvet chair. Ill health soon compelled Delaware to go back to England, and then the rude church again began to decay.

Crashaw speaks of all the clergymen who left England, as being "single men." If this statement is correct, Buck must have married some of the female passengers wrecked at Bermudas, or some one in Virginia, soon after, for in 1611 there is evidence that he was a husband. Toward the latter part of that year, in the midst of great destitution, his wife bore a daughter, which was appropriately named Mara. The mother, in her desolation, thought, no doubt, of the green hedges and good cheer of dear old England, and appreciated the language of Naomi, in the Book of Ruth—"Call me not Naomi, call me Mara, for the Almighty hath dealt very bitterly with me. I went out full, and the Lord hath brought me home again, empty."

Three years after Mara's birth the Lord gave the wife of Buck a son, which was named Gershom. The good man thought of Moses, no doubt, who, when his wife, Zipporah, bare him a son, "he called his name Gershom, for, he said, I have been a stranger in a strange land."

In the year 1616, the minister's wife became the mother of a son, which proved a child of sorrow, and was well called Benoni. He did not chuckle and laugh in childish glee, he had a vacant stare, and it was soon evident that he would not be able to measure a yard of cloth, number twenty, or rightly name the days of the week, and that he, under the English Statute, would be called "a natural fool."

The fourth child was born about the time that the first legislature met, and the colony was "pelegged," or divided into many election precincts, and the boy was named Peleg.

Mr. Buck died before the year 1624, but the precise time has not been ascertained. Ambrose Harmar, who in 1645 was a member of the legislature from Jamestown, in a petition presented in 1637, states that he had for thirteen years had the care of the idiot Benoni Buck, the first in the colony, and appears to have been the guardian of the other children.

By Buck's will, his wife had a life interest in his lands, and after her death they were to belong to the children. Hening's Statutes state that the attention of the legislature of March 1654–5 was called to the will of Richard Buck, and it was decided that his lands descended to his children, and not to Bridget Bromfield, late wife of John Burrowes, and that Elizabeth Crompe was to remain in possession.

Thomas Crompe came to Virginia as early as A.D. 1624, and was a delegate to the legislature that met in February, 1631–32, from James City. Elizabeth Crompe may have been the daughter of Thomas Crompe and Mara Buck, and the grandchild of Rev. Richard Buck.

In 1624 Mara Buck, then unmarried, was living with John and Bridget Burrowes, at James City. Could Bridget Burrowes have been the widow of Buck, and, after the death of Burrowes, could Mr. Bromfield have become a third husband?

GEORGE KEITH.

A minister named George Keith, thirty-three years of age, with a wife, and son John, aged six years, in 1617 arrived in the ship "George," and settled at Elizabeth City. He may have been the same person who was the first minister at the Bermudas, whose governor at this time was Daniel Tucker, who had been a councillor and prominent citizen of Virginia.

He entered one hundred acres, by patent, and for some time a creek in the neighborhood of Elizabeth City, now Hampton, was called Keith's.

His wife appears to have died, 1624. If he was the first minister of Bermudas, he was a nonconformist.

WILLIAM MEASE.

William Mease came about the time of Glover and Buck, remained ten years in Virginia, and in 1623 was living in England.

THOMAS BARGRAVE.

Thomas Bargrave, who came in 1618, was the nephew of Dr. Bargrave, the Dean of Canterbury, and came out with his uncle, Captain John Bargrave, who spent several thousand pounds, with a Mr. Ward, in establishing a plantation on the south side of the James, above Martin Brandon, in the district through which runs a creek, to this day called Ward's. He probably succeeded Wickham at Henrico, and Whitaker at Bermuda Hundred. He died in 1621, and left his library, valued at one hundred marks, or seventy pounds, to the projected college at Henrico.

DAVID SANDS, OR SANDYS.

David Sands, or Sandys, came in the "Bona Ventura," in 1620, and first dwelt at John Utie's plantation in Hog Island, but early in 1625 he was at the plantation of Captain Samuel Matthews, within the precincts of James City. In July, 1624, he petitioned for relief from calumny derogatory to his profession.

JONAS STOCKTON

Arrived in January, 1621, in the ship "Bona Nova," and was about thirty-six years of age. His residence was at Elizabeth City, but for a time he preached at Henrico. In January, 1625, he was alive, but after this he is not mentioned in any of the records we have examined.

Governor Yeardley, in the spring of 1619, found a "poor ruinated church" at Henrico, and at Jamestown "a church built wholly at the charge of the inhabitants of that city, of timber, being fifty foot in length and twenty foot in breadth."

In 1621 Sir Francis Wyatt became Governor, and a number of clergymen came to Virginia, but the General Assembly of 1623 stated that "divers had no orders."

ROBERT PAULET.

Robert Paulet, in July, 1621, was announced as one of the Governor's Council, and was at that time residing at Martin's Hundred. He had been engaged in 1619 to go to Southampton Hundred, founded by Tracy, Throckmorton, Thorp and others, in the triple capacity of "preacher, physician, and surgeon," and arrived in the month of December. He never took the oath of Councillor. The Virginia Company of London, in a letter dated July 22d, 1622, to Governor Wyatt writes, "Mr. Robert Paulet, the minister, was he whom the court chose to be of the Council; the adventurers of Martin's Hundred desire that he might be spared for that office, their business requiring his presence continually."

ROBERT BOLTON.

In the records of the London Company is found the following minute :—"Upon the Right Honorable the Earl of Southampton's recommendations of Mr. Bolton, minister, for his honesty and sufficiency in learning, and to undertake the care and charge of the ministry, the Company have been pleased to entertain him for their minister in some vacant place in Virginia."

Mr. Bolton came with Governor Wyatt, in October, 1621, and was sent to Elizabeth City. He was engaged by the planters of the eastern shore of the Chesapeake Bay, as their first minister, and preached for two years there, and perhaps a longer period. He may have been the Robert Bolton who, in 1609, took the degree of A. B. at Oxford.

On November 21st, 1623, Governor Wyatt issued the following :—

"WHEREAS, it is ordered that Mr. Bolton, minister, shall receive for his salary, this year, throughout all the plantations at the Eastern Shore, ten pounds of tobacco and one bushel of corn for every planter and tradesman, above the age of sixteen years, alive at the crop: these are to require Captain William Epps, commander of the said plantation, to raise the said ten pounds of tobacco and one bushel of corn," etc.

HAWTE WYATT.

Hawte Wyatt, named after his maternal grandfather, Sir W. Hawte, also came in October, 1621, in the same vessel with his brother, Gov. Wyatt. On the 16th of July, a few days after Bolton's appointment, it was signified to the London Company that Sir Francis Wyatt's brother, "being a Master of Arts, and a good divine, and very willing to go with him this present voyage, might be entertained and placed as Minister over his people, and have the same allowance towards the furnishing of himself with necessaries, as others have had; and that his wife might have her transport free, which motive was thought very reasonable," and it was ordered that he should have the same allowance as that which had been granted to Mr. Bolton.

It is probable that the minister's wife went back in the summer of 1623, as a companion of the Governor's wife, and in 1626 he came to England, his father having died. Upon his return to England he found a great deal of ecclesiastical controversy, and his sympathies were with the Puritans. Opposed to the retrogressions of Archbishop Laud, he was arraigned before the High Commission. On the 3d of October he became Vicar of Bexley, Kent, the seat of his ancestors. He was twice married, and on the 31st of July, 1638, died. Some of his descendants came back to Virginia. Anthony Wyatt, one of Governor Berkeley's councillors in 1642, may have been his son, and perhaps Ralph Wyatt, who married the widow of Captain William Button, a gentleman who had received from the Privy Council of England a grant of 7000 acres on both sides of the river Appomattox.

WILLIAM BENNETT.

About the same time, in 1621, that Hawte Wyatt came, arrived William Bennett, in the ship "Sea Flower." He preached at the plantation settled under the auspices of Edward Bennett, a prominent London merchant, in the Warosquoyak district, which extended on the south side of James river. There is a warrant dated November 20th, 1623, for collecting of the estate of Robert Bennett the salary of William Bennett for two years.

His wife came in the "Abigail," in July, 1622, and shortly after his marriage, toward the close of the year 1624, he died.

On the 22d of January, 1624–5, Catharine, the widow of the minister, aged twenty-four, was residing at Shirley, with William, her infant, three weeks old.

THOMAS WHITE.

In December, 1621, Thomas White arrived in the ship Warwick. Governor Wyatt and Council, in a letter to the London Company, written the next month, uses these words:—"The information given you of the want of worthy ministers here is very true, and therefore we must give you great thanks for sending out Mr. Thomas White. It is our earnest request that you would be pleased to send us out many more learned and sincere ministers, of which there is so great want in so many parts of the country."

White appears to have died before 1624, and his place of residence in the colony has not been ascertained.

WILLIAM LEATE OR LEAKE.

Humphry Slany, one of the prominent merchants of London, at one of the meetings of the London Company in 1622, informed them that Mr. Leate, a man of "civil and good carriage," formerly a preacher in New Foundland, was desirous to go to Virginia, and would put the Company to no charge, except for necessaries and such books as should be useful to him. A committee conferred with him, and asked him to preach on a certain Sunday, in the afternoon, on the second verse of the 9th chapter of Isaiah, at Saint Scythe's Church, which was surrounded by handsome mansions in Saint Swithen's lane, near London Stone.

He appears to have made a favorable impression. In a letter to the colonial authorities, the Company write, on 10th of July, 1622, O. S.:—"We send over Mr. William Leate, a minister recommended unto us for sufficiency of learning and integrity of life." In less than six months he died. Governor Wyatt, the next January, wrote: "The little experience we have of Mr. Leate made good your commendations of him, and his death to us very grievous."

GREVILLE POOLEY.

Greville Pooley arrived in the ship "James," in 1622, and resided on the south side of James river, at Fleur-dieu Hundred, one of Governor Yeardley's plantations, adjoining Jordan's plantation.

Samuel Jordan, a few months after Pooley's arrival, died, and the burial service was conducted by the neighboring minister. He left a young widow about twenty-three years of age, named Cecilia, called Siselye, and a daughter Mary, two years of age, and Margaret, an infant.

Pooley asserted that a few days after the funeral he courted the widow, and was encouraged, but afterward she accepted the attentions of William Ferrar, a neighbor, and brother of the Deputy Governor of the Virginia Company in London. The affair caused a great deal of gossip, and Governor Wyatt referred Pooley's complaint of breach of promise to the London Company. In the Company's *Transactions* is the following minute, under date of April 21st, 1624: "Papers were read, whereof one containing certain examinations touching a difference between Mr. Pooley and Mrs. Jordan, referred unto the Company here for answer, and the Court requested to confer with some civilians, and advise what answer was fit to be returned in such a case." A few months later the Governor of Virginia issued the following order against flirting: "Whereas, to the great contempt of the majesty of God and ill example to others, certain women within this colony have, of late, contrary to the laws ecclesiastical of the realm of England, contracted themselves to two several men at one time, whereby much trouble doth grow between parties, and the Governor and Council of State much disquieted. To prevent the like offense to others hereafter, it is by the Governor and Council ordered in Court that every minister give notice in his church, to his parishioners, that what man or woman soever shall use any words or speech tending to the contract of marriage, though not right and legal, yet so may entangle and breed struggle in their consciences, shall for the third offense undergo either corporal punishment, or other punishment by fine or otherwise, according to the guilt of the persons so offending."

Poor Pooley at last found a woman to love and be his wife, but in 1629 he and his family were massacred by the Indians.

MR. FENTON.

At Elizabeth City, on the 5th of September, 1624, a Rev. Mr. Fenton was buried, who had recently arrived.

HENRY JACOB.

Henry Jacob, the eminent scholar and writer, and founder of the first Independent Church in London, was induced to come to Virginia, about 1624, and soon died. It is supposed that he may have gone to the Puritan plantations of Warasquoyak, established by Edward Bennett and other London merchants, and perhaps succeeded William Bennett.

CHAPTER III.

CLERGY FROM A.D. 1630 TO A.D. 1660.

WILLIAM COTTON.

William Cotton is the second minister residing on the eastern shore of Chesapeake Bay, and may have been the immediate successor of Robert Bolton, whom we have noticed. It was a law of the colony "that whosoever should disparage a minister without sufficient proof to justify his reports, whereby the minds of his parishioners might be alienated from him, and his ministry prove the less effectual, should ask the minister forgiveness, publicly, in the congregation."

Henry Charlton, who, at the age of nineteen, came in 1623 to Virginia, and was a servant of a planter in Accomac, Captain John Wilcocks, one day in 1633 called the Rev. Mr. Cotton "a black-coated rascal," and it was ordered by the County Court, "that Mr. Henry Charlton make a pair of stocks, and sit in them several Sabbath days, during divine service, and then ask Mr. Cotton's forgiveness for using offensive and slanderous words concerning him."

Stephen Charlton, who left, on certain conditions, property to the Episcopal Church in Northampton, or lower Accomac, was probably the son of this offender.

MR. FALKNER.

Mr. Falkner, in the proceedings of the Assembly of 1643, is mentioned as the rector of the large parish of the Isle of Wight county, but we find no further record of his life.

It was not until after the year 1630 that the colonists of Virginia began to increase in wealth and population. In May, 1630, the population of the Colony was reputed to be twenty-five hundred. But in five years it had doubled. In 1636 twenty-six ships arrived, bringing sixteen hundred and six immigrants. After this period there was some improvement in architecture.

The Virginia planters, in a document written in 1623, state "that the houses were most built for use and not for ornament." The laboring men's houses in England, to which class they say "We chiefly profess ourselves to be, are in no wise generally, for goodness, to be compared unto them."

To stimulate improvements, in 1638 the authorities at Jamestown offered land for a house and garden to any who would build a dwelling.

In 1640 twelve houses were built, one of brick, owned by Secretary Kemp, and considered the "fairest in the Colony," and at the same time the first brick church in Virginia, twenty-eight by fifty-six feet in size, was commenced at Jamestown. Many years afterwards, A. D. 1676, it was destroyed by fire, and another church, the ruins of which are still seen, was erected.

A levy of tobacco, at the same period, was ordered, to repair Point Comfort and build a State-house at Jamestown, and Menefie, sometimes spelled Menify, a prominent merchant, was sent to England to dispose of the tobacco and procure workmen.

ANTHONY PANTON.

Anthony Panton was the most prominent of the Virginia clergy, from the beginning of the reign of Charles the First until the death of Charles the Second.

At the solicitation of George Menify, a prominent man in Virginia affairs, and others, Panton, in 1633, came to America.

Menify had arrived in July, 1623, in the ship "Samuel," and became, in a few years, a prosperous merchant of James City corporation, and agent for London merchants. He lived on a plantation called Littleton, between Jamestown and Warwick river, and his surroundings were more refined than the other colonists. He was the first person who raised peach trees in the valley of James river, and gave great attention to horticulture. His garden of two acres was full of primroses, sage, marjoram and rosemary, and also contained apple, cherry, pear and peach trees. Panton's field of labor was in the new plantation of York, and the parish of Chiskiak, created 1639–40 by the legislature.

In 1629 a law relative to the observance of the Sabbath was rëenacted in these words: 'That there be an especiall care taken by all commanders and others that the people doe repaire to their churches on the Saboth day, and to see that the penalty of one pound of tobacco for every time of absence, and fifty pound of tobacco for every month's absence, sett down in the act of the Generall Assembly, 1623, be levyed, and the delinquents to pay the same, as also to see that the Saboth day be not ordinarily profaned by working in any imployments, or by iourneying from place to place."

About the time of Panton's arrival, in view of the scarcity of ministers, the legislature enacted: "In such places where the extent of the care of any mynister is so large that he cannot be present himself on the Saboth dayes and other holy dayes, It is thought fitt, That they appoynt and allow mayntenance for deacons, where any having taken orders can be found, for the readinge common prayer in their absence."

The Virginians had been indignant at the intrusion of Governor Calvert upon one of their plantations in Chesapeake bay, which had sent a representative to the legislature at Jamestown, and when one of their citizens, of the isle of Kent, had been killed in a collision with Marylanders, they became indignant at Governor Harvey's sympathy with those whom they considered intruders, and on the 27th of April, 1635, a meeting of influential persons was held at the York plantations, to adopt measures of redress for the many grievances they had suffered from their Governor. The next day a meeting of the Council was held at Jamestown, and after excited discussion, Governor Harvey was arrested for treason, and sent over to England. The following December, at a meeting of the king's Privy Council, it was charged that one Rabnet, of

Maryland, had said that it was lawful and meritorious to kill a heretic king, which was offered to be proved by one Mr. Williams, a minister, but Governor Harvey refused his testimony, because he married two persons without a license.

Another charge was that he had silenced a minister by the name of White.

To this Governor Harvey answered that White, in two years' time, had never shown any orders.

Archbishop Laud, who was present at the examination, sustained Harvey, by saying, "that no man may be admitted to serve as a Minister in any of the King's ships, until he has shown his orders to the Bishop of the Diocese."

Harvey was upheld by the King, and reäppeared in Jamestown in 1637, with increased authority, and the increased dislike of the Virginians. The Secretary of the Colony and warm sympathizer with the Governor was Richard Kemp.

Acting both as accuser and judge, in 1638, Kemp charged Anthony Panton, Rector of York and Chiskiack, with calling him "a jackanapes; that the King was misinformed, and that he was unfit for the place of Secretary, that he was poor and proud, with hair-lock tied up with a ribbon as old as Paul's," and also that he had preached against his pride; upon these charges, Harvey banished the minister for "mutinous, rebellious and riotous actions."

Panton complained to the King's Privy Council. Harvey was soon removed from office and his successor, Governor Wyatt, was ordered to inquire into the Panton difficulty.

Before he could enter upon the examination, Kemp, without permission, sailed for England, and Thomas Stegg, of Westover, an influential merchant, who was once Speaker of the Assembly, was fined 50 pounds sterling and to be imprisoned during the Governor's pleasure, for aiding and assisting him to go out of the country, and furnishing him with money, because it endangered the colonial records, some of which he had carried away, and because he exhibited contempt toward the Governor in refusing to answer Panton's counsel. In April, 1641, the Privy Council having heard both Kemp and Panton, the sentence against the minister was removed. On the 30th of October, Anthony Panton, calling himself "Clerk and Minister of God's Word in Virginia, and Agent of the Church and Clergy there," presented a petition to the House of Lords, in which he complained of the conduct of Governor Harvey, Secretary Richard Kemp and others, at whose hands the colonists had suffered many arbitrary and illegal proceedings, in speedy trial, extortionate and most cruel oppressions which have extended to unjust whippings, cutting of ears, fines, confinement of honest men's goods, peculation, and the supporting of Popery. He also stated that Kemp had secretly fled from Virginia, carrying away the charter and divers records, and with his associates had, by misrepresentations to his Majesty relative to Governor Francis Wyatt, who had only served under his last commission eighteen months, obtained a new government and a new charter.

After the reading of these complaints, it was ordered by the House of Lords that the new Governor, Sir W. Berkeley, Kt., Richard Kemp and Christopher Wormsley be stayed their voyage, and forthwith answer to the charges of the petitioner. Berkeley's commission as Governor had been signed in August, but owing to this and other delays he did not, before February, 1642, enter upon his duties in Virginia.

JAMES, KNOWLES, AND TOMPSON, PURITANS.

While Laud in England was having the "Book of Sports" read in the churches, and the youth, on Sunday afternoons, were encouraged to engage in games and dances, and the Court on Sunday evenings were at balls, plays, and masquerades, the Virginia Legislature, in March, 1643, enacted: "For the better observation of the Saboth, no person or persons shall take a voyage upon the same, except it be to Church, or for other cause of extreme necessitie, upon the penaltie of the forfeiture, for such offence, of twenty pounds."

It had already, in 1629, been ordered "that the Saboth day be not ordinarily profaned by workeing in any imployments."

The assembly of 1643 provided for the spiritual independence of the parishes outside of James City, by a law, which gave to the vestry of a parish and the county commissioners the right to elect and make choice of their ministers, which ministers should not be suspended by the Governor, except by complaint made by the vestry, and that final removal from the parish pulpit was to be left to the Legislature.

In the summer of 1641 the minister of the large parish of Upper Norfolk, afterward Nansemond county, signified his intention to leave. In May, 1642, a letter was written and signed by Richard Bennett, Daniel Gookin, John Hill, and others, "to the pastors and elders of Christ Church in New England," which was carried to Boston by Philip Bennett, one of the best men of Virginia, and contained a request for three pastors to occupy parishes which had been created by the legislature a few weeks before.

The act was in these words: "For the better enabling the inhabitants of this colony to the religious worship and service of Almighty God, which is often neglected and slackened by the inconvenient and remote vastness of parishes,

"*Resolved*, That the county of Upper Norfolk be divided into three distinct parishes, viz't.: one on the south side of Nansimum river, from the present glebe to head of said river, on the other side of the river the bounds to be limited from Cooling's Creek, including both sides of the creek, upward to the head of the western branch, and to be nominated the South Parish.

"It is also thought and confirmed that the east side of Nansimum river, from present glebe downward to the north of said river be a peculiar parish, to which the glebe and parsonage house that now is shall be appropriated and called East Parish. The third parish to begin on the west side of Nansimum river, to be limited from Cooling's creek, as aforesaid, and to extend downward to the mouth of the river, including all Chuckatuck on both sides, and the Ragged Islands, to be known by the West Parish."

The request was prayerfully considered by the churches and ministers of Boston and vicinity, and three good men offered themselves—John Knowles, pastor at Watertown, and a ripe scholar from Immanuel, Cambridge; William Tompson, minister at Braintree, who had graduated at Oxford in 1619; and Thomas James, for two years the minister at Charlestown, and then removed to New Haven.

Early in 1643 they arrived at Jamestown, bearing a letter of introduction from Governor Winthrop to Governor Berkeley. They were coldly received, and Thomas Harrison, as Chaplain, used his influence to have them silenced, and thus prevented from preaching in the churches; but Winthrop, in his journal, says, "Though the State did silence the ministers because they would not conform to the order of England, yet the people resorted to them in private houses, to hear them."

Knowles and James returned after a few months, but Tompson, of "tall and comely presence," remained longer." Mather, in a commemorative poem, alludes to his success in Virginia—

"A constellation of great converts there
Shone round him, and his heavenly glory
wear;
Gookin was one of them; by Tompson's
pains,
Christ and New England a dear Gookin
gains."

Daniel Gookin was the son of the Daniel Gookin, of County Cork, Ireland, who in 1621 commenced a plantation at Newport's News. The father and son were both natives of Kent County, England. In 1637

Daniel Gookin, Sr., obtained a grant of twenty-five hundred acres upon the branch of Nansemond river, and in 1642 he was president of the county court there, and one of those who invited the ministers from New England, and by Tompson's preaching his son Daniel, about twenty-five years old, became a member of the Church, and in 1644 went to Boston to reside. Here he became a man of influence, a friend of Eliot, the missionary and superintendent of Indian affairs. He died in March, 1687, aged seventy-five years, and his tombstone is still seen in the graveyard at Cambridge. Sewall, the Chief Justice of Massachusetts, visited him when dying; in his diary he calls him "a right good man." His descendants were very numerous.

THOMAS HARRISON, D.D.

Thomas Harrison first appears in Virginia as the chaplain of Governor Berkeley.

He was a man of learning, eloquence and pathos, and upon his arrival a strict conformist to the Canons and liturgy of the Church of England.

On the 13th of April, 1644, there was a naval engagement between a ship whose captain adhered to the cause of Charles the First, and two ships whose officers were in sympathy with Parliament. The divisions and strifes caused by the civil war in England had been noticed by the Indians, and on the 18th, a black Good Friday in the Colonial calendar, the savages suddenly swarmed around the feeble settlements in the Valley of the James River, and as quickly disappeared, with their hands full of reeking scalps. Strong men fainted with horror, some mourned and refused to be comforted, for their children were not, and all felt it was a heavy judgment.

From this time Harrison was a changed man. His sermons became more solemn and spiritual. He expressed his regret that, while keeping a fair exterior to the ministers from New England, he had quietly used his influence to have them silenced.

The Act passed by the legislature soon after the massacre had his full sympathy, and indicates a reviving of religious life. It is as follows:—

"*Be it enacted by the Governour, Counsell, and Burgesses of this present Grand Assembly*, for God's glory, and the publick benefitt of the Collony, to the end that God might avert his heavie judgments that are now upon us, That the last Wednesday be sett apart for a day of ffast and humiliation, And that it be wholly dedicated to prayers and preaching, And because of the scarcity of pastors, many ministers having charge of two cures,

"Be it enacted, that such a minister shall officiate in one cure upon the last Wednesday of everie month; and in his other upon the first Wednesday of the ensuing month, And in case of haveing three cures, that hee officiate in his third cure upon the second Wednesday of the ensuing month, which shall be their day of fast; That the last act, made the 11 of January, 1641, concerning the ministers preaching in the forenoon and catechiseing in the afternoon of every Sunday, be revived and stand in force, And in case any minister do faile so to doe, That he forfeit 500 pounds of tobaccoe, to be disposed of by the vestrey for use of the parish."

The arbitrary and choleric Berkeley disliked Harrison's changed manner, and dismissed him, as too grave a Chaplain. He then crossed over to the parishes of Nansemond, whose ministers he had helped to drive away, and preached to the people.

In October, 1645, the House of Commons ordered that there should be liberty of conscience, in matters of God's worship, in all of the American plantations. The next year Captain Sayle, afterward Governor of Carolina, and the venerable Patrick Copland, in his youth the friend of Nicholas Ferrar, and a preacher before the London Company in 1622, of a sermon which was printed with the title "Virginia's God be Thanked," left Bermudas with a party of sympathizers, and sailed to Eleuthera, a small isle of the Bahamas group, to establish a colony, where each person was to be at perfect liberty to worship as he pleased, without molestation from the State. The ship in which they embarked, when near their destination, struck upon a reef, and they lost much of their supplies. As soon as possible Captain Sayle built a pinnace, and with eight men steered for Virginia, and arrived there in nine days, and received succor from the Nansemond nonconformists. Finding that Governor Berkeley was bitterly opposed to Puritanism, Sayle proposed to Harrison that his parishioners should cast in their lot with Copland and others at Eleuthera, but the proposition was not accepted.

Among the "Winthrop Papers" there is a letter of Harrison, written at Elizabeth River, on the 2d of November, 1646, and sent to Boston by Captain Edward Gibbons, "the younger brother of the house of an honorable extraction," in which he writes that if the proposition had "found us risen up in a posture of removal, there is weight and force enough [in yours] to have staked us down again."

After this the Nansemond Puritans, upon the express condition that there would be a public legal acknowledgment of toleration in religion, migrated to Maryland and settled on the shores of the Chesapeake, near Annapolis. Harrison, in the fall of 1648, visited Boston, married a cousin of Governor Winthrop, one Dorothy Symonds, and returned to England.

On October 11th, 1649, the Council of State wrote to Governor Berkeley that they were informed by petition of the congregation of Nansemond, that their minister, Mr. Harrison, an able man of unblamable conversation, had been banished the colony because he would not conform to the use of the Common Prayer-book, and as he could not be ignorant that the use of it was prohibited by Parliament, he was directed to allow Mr. Harrison to return to the ministry.

Harrison did not return to America, but became Chief Chaplain of Henry Cromwell, Lord Lieutenant of Ireland, and in Christ Church Cathedral, Dublin, he preached a sermon on the death of Oliver Cromwell, from the text, Lamentations, chapter v, verse 16th, which was published with the following title:—

"*Threni Hibernici; or, Ireland sympathizing with England and Scotland in a sad lamentation for the loss of their Josiah. Represented in a sermon at Christ Church, in Dublin, before his Excellency the Lord Deputy, with divers of the nobility, gentry and commonality there assembled, to celebrate a funeral solemnity, upon the death of the Lord Protector, by Dr. Harrison, Chief Chaplain to his said Excellency.*"

THOMAS HAMPTON.

Thomas Hampton seems to have been the successor of Harrison at Jamestown; and in "Hening's Statutes" he is mentioned as consenting, in February, 1645, to the formation of a new parish called Harrope, including the Williamsburgh region. At a later period Wallingford was also set off from the old parish. Upon an old tombstone at Williamsburgh Bishop Meade found this inscription:—"The Rev. Thomas Hampton, Rector of this parish, in 1647."

ROBERT BRACEWELL.

Robert Bracewell was elected a burgess to the Assembly of 1653, but it was ordered "that Mr. Robert Bracewell, Clerk, be suspended, and is not in a capacity of serving as a Burgess since, since it was unpresidential, and may produce bad consequences."

The obstacles to his taking a seat in the legislature cannot be ascertained. John Hammond, for seventeen years a resident of Virginia, in 1652 represented the Isle of Wight County in the Assembly, was expelled from that body and the colony, for libel and other illegal practices, and then went to Maryland, and from thence to England, where he appeared as a partisan pamphleteer in defense of Lord Baltimore and his officers in Maryland.

In a publication called "Leah and Rachel," which appeared in 1656, and is reprinted in the Force Historical Tracts, he writes: "But Virginia, savouring not handsomely in England, very few of good conversation would adventure thither, as thinking it a place where the fear of God was not; yet many came, such as wore black coats, and could babble in a pulpit, roar in a tavern, exact from the parishioners, and rather, by their dissoluteness, destroy than feed their flocks."

He continued: "The country was loth to be wholly without teachers, and therefore rather retain these than to be destitute; yet still endeavors for better in their places, which were obtained, and these wolves in sheep's clothing, by their Assemblies were questioned, silenced, and some forced to depart the country."

ROGER GREEN.

In July, 1653, Roger Green, minister of Nansemond, is spoken of as contemplating a journey to North Carolina. Francis Yeardley this year was a representative of Lower Norfolk County in the Legislature, and Green probably accompanied his brother, Argall Yeardley, this year, in his explorations to the Roanoke region. The Yeardleys were sons of the former Governor, and, as the Nansemond people, were Puritan in their sympathies.

PHILIP MALLORY.

As early as the year 1644 a Mr. Mallory was rector of Hampton. In Hening's Statutes is the following Act of 1656:—"For the encouragement of the ministers in the country, and that they may be the better enabled to attend both public commands and their private cures, It is ordered, that from henceforth each minister, in his owne person, with six other servants of his family, shall be free from publique levies, Allwaies provided they be examined by Mr. Philip Mallory and Mr. John Green, and they do certify their abilities to the Governour and Councill, who are to proceed according to their judgement." The Assembly of March, 1660–61 enacted, "Whereas, Mr. Philip Mallory hath been eminently faithfull in the ministry, and very diligent in endeavouring the advancement of all those meanes that might conduce to the advancement of religion in this country, *It is ordered,* that he be desired to undertake the soliciting of our church affaires in England, and there be paid him a gratuity for the many pains he hath alreadie and hereafter is like to take about the countrey's business, the sum of eleven thousand pounds of tobacco." In 1664 he was still rector of Hampton parish.

SAMUEL COLE.

About the year 1650, in the absence of any vestry, Samuel Cole, Bishop Meade says, was appointed minister in one of the new counties of the Potomac, by the County Court. In 1657 Mr. Cole was minister to the two parishes in Middlesex County.

FRANCIS DOUGHTY.

Francis Doughty is mentioned as having preached in Lower Accomac, now Northampton. He was the brother-in-law of Willliam Stone, of Hungar's parish, who became the first Protestant governor of Maryland, and introduced the Puritans of Virginia to the shores of the Chesapeake in 1648, on condition that there was a law passed securing liberty of conscience.

Francis Doughty first lived in New England, then went to Long Island, and while there used to preach to the English in Manhattan, now New York City. His wife was the widow of Rev. John Moore.

After Stone became governor, Doughty resided in Maryland, and on Sunday, October 12, 1659, visited the Dutch Commissioners from Manhattan, who were dining at Philip Calvert's house.

The only letter extant of John Washington is one dated September 30, 1659, in which he tells the Governor of Maryland that he cannot attend the October Court at St. Mary, "because then, God willing, I intend to get my young son baptized. All of ye company and gossips being already invited."

Perhaps Doughty crossed the Potomac to perform the baptismal act for one of the pioneers of Westmoreland, Virginia.

Doughty's daughter first married Adrian Vanderdonk, a graduate of Leyden, a lawyer at Manhattan. After his death she became a wife of Hugh O'Neal, a planter on the Patuxent River, Maryland.

The Rev. Mr. Doughty at one time preached in Setlingbourne Parish, about ten miles from the plantation of John Washington, and there is extant a complaint against him, presented to the Governor by John Catlett and Humphrey Boothe, for refusing to allow them "to communicate in the blessed ordinance of the Lord's Supper," in which the complainants state that Doughty is a "nonconformist," and that on a certain occasion "he denied the supremacy of the king, contrary to the canons of the Church of England." A century later one George Washington, a relative of one of Doughty's parishioners, also denied the supremacy of the king.

CHAPTER IV.

CLERGY FROM A.D. 1660 TO A.D. 1688.

Virginia, from the death of Oliver Cromwell until the accession of William and Mary to the throne of England, was largely given up to ignorance and riotous living. Berkeley was again made Governor in A. D. 1660, and retained the position until A. D. 1677. He hated the restraints of religion, indulged in profanity, and was the companion of the pleasure-loving Charles the Second. Having ejected hundreds of clergymen of Puritan sympathies from the pulpits of England, there were many vacancies for strict conformists to the Prayer-book, and few desired to go to the forests of America. Governor Berkeley's dislike of nonconformist ministers was also so great that they could not live in Virginia without molestation.

To the question of the English Government, propounded in 1671, "what course is taken about the instructing the people within your Government in the Christian religion, and what provision is there made for the paying of your ministry?" Berkeley bluntly replied, "We have forty-eight parishes, and our ministers are well paid, and by my consent, would be better, if they would pray oftener and preach less. But, as of all other commodities, so, of this, *the worst are sent us*, and we had few that we would boast of, since the persecution of Cromwell's tyranny drove divers worthy men hither. But I thank God there are no free schools, nor printing; and I hope we shall not have, these hundred years; for learning has brought disobedience, and heresy, and sects into the world, and printing has divulged them and libels against the Government."

With a Governor and clergymen that did not command the respect of good men, yet laying stress upon the efficacy of its ordinances of baptism and the Lord's Supper, it is not strange that religious people began to hold meetings in their own houses, and place a low estimate upon any kind of ritualism, and listen to the preachers of the Society of Friends.

In 1663, John Porter was expelled from the House of Burgesses, because, in the language of the Act, he had been "loving to the Friends."

GEORGE WILSON, FRIEND.

The itinerant ministry of the Society of Friends, visiting from plantation to plantation, neatly attired, temperate in the use of meat and drink, appealing only to the New Testament, could but make a favorable impression upon the fair-minded; while it stirred up formalists of the Colony, to cause the passage of a law, ordering "that all Quakers, for assembling in unlawful assemblages and conventicles, shall be fined, and pay, each of them there taken, two hundred pounds of tobacco."

George Wilson, a minister of the Society of Friends from England, was imprisoned, and there is preserved a letter, dated, "From that dirty dungeon in James Town, the 17th of the Third Month, 1662," in which he writes, "If they who visit not such in prison as Christ speaks of, shall be punished with everlasting destruction, O! what will ye do? or what will become of you, who put us into such nasty, stinking prisons as this dirty dungeon, where we have not had the benefit to do what nature requireth, nor so much as air to blow in at the window, but close made up with brick and lime?"

R. G., PERHAPS, ROGER GREEN.

About the time that the Colonial authorities were holding Friends, in Jamestown prison, a small quarto was published in London, in 1662, under the signature of R. G., entitled "*Virginia's Cure; or an Advisive Concerning Virginia, Discovering the True Ground of that Church's Unhappiness.*" The writer thereof states that he had been for ten years a resident of Virginia, and he was, perhaps, Roger Green, who in Henry's Statutes is mentioned, in 1653, as Minister in Nansemond. R. G., in 1661, had returned to England, and in his pamphlet, the importance of concentrating the population of Virginia in two, the establishment of Fellowship in Oxford and Cambridge, for the supply of an educated ministry, and the appointment of a Bishop for Virginia, are earnestly urged. His representations made an impression, and a patent for the creation of a Bishop was drawn, and the Rev. Alexander Murray was nominated for the office, but difficulties arose, and the scheme was abandoned.

Speaking of the members of the Virginia Assembly, R. G. writes, they were "usually such as went over servants thither, and though by time and industry they may have attained competent estates, yet, by reason of their poor and mean condition, were unskillful in judging of a good estate, either of Church or Commonwealth, or the means of procuring it."

The immodest and immoral poetess, Aphra Behn, who lived at this period, in one of her plays, alludes to the above state of things, by introducing two friends at Jamestown, who converse as follows:—

"*Hazard.* This unexpected happiness o'erjoys! who could have imagined to have found thee in Virginia!

"*Friend.* My uncle's dying here left me a considerable plantation, * * * * * but pr'ythee what drew thee to this part of the new world?

"*Hazard.* Why, faith, ill company, and the common vice of the town, gaming. * * * * * I had rather starve abroad, than live pitied and despised at home.

"*Friend.* Would he [the new Governor] were landed; we hear he is a noble gentleman.

"*Hazard.* He has all the qualities of a gentleman; besides, he is nobly born.

"*Friend.* This country wants nothing but to be peopled with a well-born race, to make it one of the best colonies in the world, * * * * * but we are ruled by a Council, some of which have been, perhaps, transported criminals, who having now acquired great estates, are now become your Honor, and R't. Worshipful, and possess all places."

MORGAN GODWYN OR GODWIN.

Morgan Godwyn came to Virginia after the publication, and perhaps was stirred to leave his warm nest in England by the reading, of R. G.'s pamphlet. He was an earnest young student, about twenty years of age, when the essay was published, and belonged to a family of theologians. His great-grandfather was the learned Thomas Godwyn, Bishop of Bath and Wells. His grandfather, Francis, was the Bishop of Hereford, and his father, Morgan, Archdeacon of Shropshire. He entered Oxford in 1661, and received, on March 16th, 1664–5, the degree of A. B., and soon after came to Virginia. His residence in the Colony was not pleasant. He was horrified at the state of morals, and the abject condition of the Africans and Indians, who were treated with less consideration than the dogs of a planter's kennel. Returning to England, after sojourning for some time in the West Indies, he engaged in the crusade against slaveholders, which a century later was taken up by Clarkson and Wilberforce. In 1680 he published a dissertation called "*The Negroes' and Indians' Advocate suing for their admission into the Church, or a Persuasive to the instructing and baptizing the Negroes and Indians in our Plantations; showing that as the compliance therewith can prejudice no man's just interest, so the willful and neglectful opposing of it is no less a manifest apostasy from the Christian Faith.*"

Five years later he preached a discourse in Westminster Abbey, exposing the inhumanity of slaveholding, from the text, Jeremiah ii, 34. "In thy skirts is found the blood of the souls of the poor innocents: I have not found it by secret search, but upon all these." It was printed under the title of "*Trade preferred before Religion, and Christ made to give place to Mammon, represented in a Sermon relating to Plantations.*"

Under his influence, it is supposed that the law was passed by the Virginia Assembly of 1667, declaring that the baptism of slaves did not make them freemen; in order that, in the language of the Act, "divers masters, freed from this doubt, may more carefully endeavor the propagation of Christianity by permitting children, though slaves, or those of greater growth, if capable, to be admitted to that sacrament."

His description of religion in Virginia is startling. He writes "The ministers are most miserably handled by the plebeian juntos, the Vestries, to whom the hiring (that is the usual word there) and admission of ministers is solely left. And there being no law obliging them to procure any more than a lay reader, to be obtained at a very moderate rate, they either resolve to have none at all, or to reduce them to their own terms." In another place he asserts: "Two-thirds of the preachers are made up of leaden lay-priests of the vestries' ordination, and are both the shame and grief of the rightly ordained clergy there."

THOMAS TEACKLE.

Thomas Teackle was the son of a royalist, who was killed in the war between Charles and the Parliament. He came to Virginia in 1656, and settled at Cradock, in lower Accomac, now Northampton County. He married Margaret, daughter of Robert Nelson, a merchant of London, and remained in that county until the day of his death, January 26, 1695. His son John, born September 2, 1693, married, in 1710, a daughter of Arthur Upshur, a gentleman whose house was open for Friends' preachers. The descendants of this early Virginia clergyman are wide-spread. The writer values the acquaintance of one of them, a lady of quiet culture and retiring disposition, one of whose parents was a Teackle, of Virginia, the other a lineal descendant of a graduate of Trinity College, Cambridge, Old England, and an early President of Harvard University, at Cambridge, in New England.

EDMUNDSON, THE FRIEND.

William Edmundson, once a soldier in Cromwell's army, came to the Chesapeake with George Fox, the great leader among the Society of Friends. While the latter visited New England, Edmundson traveled in North Carolina and Virginia. In 1672 he visited Governor Berkeley, and in his Journal writes:—

"As I returned, it was laid upon me to visit the Governor, Sir William Berkeley, and to speak with him about Friends' sufferings. I went about six miles out of my way to speak with him, accompanied by William Garrett, an honest, ancient Friend. I told the Governor I came from Ireland, where his brother was Lord Lieutenant, who was so kind to our Friends, and if he had any service to his brother, I would willingly do it; and as his brother was kind to our Friends in Ireland, I hoped he would be so to our Friends in Virginia. He was very peevish and brittle, and I could fasten nothing on him with all the soft arguments I could use."

JOHN CLOUGH OR CLUFF.

John Cluff was one of the ministers denounced by young Nathaniel Bacon in the civil war of 1676, for upholding Governor Berkeley. In the year 1680 he was Rector of Southwark, in Surry County.

JOHN PAGE.

John Page was another clergyman denounced in 1676 by Bacon. In 1680 he had charge of all the churches in Elizabeth County. In 1687 he was in New Kent County, and in 1719 he was still alive and in Elizabeth County.

MR. WADING.

When Bacon led the insurgents to Gloucester County, a minister named Wading refused to acknowledge his authority, and encouraged others to follow his example. Bacon placed him under arrest, telling him that it was his place to preach in the Church and not in the camp. In the Church he could say what he pleased, but in the camp he was to say no more than what should please Bacon, unless he would fight to better purpose than he could preach. The second in command under Major Laurence Smith, during the Bacon insurrection, was a minister, who, says a chronicler of the day, "had laid down the miter, and taken up the helmet."

DUELL PEAD.

On the 16th of April, 1663, in the Westminster Abbey font, then newly set up, Duell Pead, one of the King's scholars, about sixteen years of age, was publicly baptized. He entered, in 1664, Trinity College, Cambridge. Ordained by the Bishop of Lincoln, in 1671, he was chaplain of H. M. Ship Rupert. In 1683 he came to Virginia, with Major General Robert Smith, remained seven years as a minister in Middlesex County, and then went back to England, and became minister of St. James, Clerkenwell. He died on the 12th of January, 1726, and was buried in the parish churchyard. He had a son, Duell, a graduate of Sidney College, Cambridge, in 1712, who became a minister and came to America. By the will of the senior Pead, some horses and cows were left to his old parish in Virginia.

JOHN CLAYTON.

Buck, Harrison, Hampton, and Godwin, have been noticed as ministers at Jamestown. By a law of the colony, the appointment of a rector for this place was made by the Governor. Godwin asserts that, with brief intervals, Jamestown for twenty years was without a rector.

About the time that Godwin was preparing his discourse in England, on "Trade before Religion," John Clayton was the parson at James City. The following letter was addressed by him to the Christian philosopher, Robert Boyle:—

"VIRGINIA, JAMES CITY, June 23d, 1684.

"HON. AND WORTHY SIR:—In England, having perused, among the rest of your valuable treatises, that ingenious discourse of the Noctiluca, wherein, as I remember, you gave an account of several nocturnal irradiations; having, therefore, met with the relation of a strange account in that nature, from very good hands, I presumed this might not prove unwelcome, for the fuller confirmation of which I have enclosed the very paper Col. Digges gave me thereof, under his own hand and name, to attest the truth, the same being likewise asserted to me by Madam Digges, his lady, sister to the said Susanna Sewell, daughter to the late Lord Baltimore, lately gone for England, who I suppose may give you fuller satisfaction of such particulars as you may be desirous to be informed of.

"I cannot but admire the strangeness of

such a complicated spirit of a volatile salt and exalted oil, as I deem it to be, from its crepitation and shining flame; how it shall transpire through the pores, and not be inflamed by the joint motion and heat of the body, and afterward so suddenly be actinated into sparks, by the slacking or bursting of her coat, raises my wonder.

"Another thing, I am confident your honor would be much pleased at the sight of a fly we have here, called the fire-fly, about the bigness of the cantharides; its body of a dark color, the tail of it a deep yellow by day, which by night shines brighter than the glow-worm, which bright shining ebbs and flows, as if the fly breathed with a bright and shining spirit. I pulled the tail of the fly into several pieces, and every parcel thereof would shine for several hours, and cast a light around it.

"Be pleased favorably to interpret this fond impertinency of a stranger. All your works have to the world evidenced your goodness, which has encouraged the presumption, which is that which bids me hope its pardon. If there be anything in this country I may please you in, be pleased to command; it will be my ambition to serve you, nor shall I scruple to ride two or three hundred miles to satisfy any query you shall propound.

"If you honor me with your commands, you may direct your letters to Mr. John Clayton, parson of James City, Virginia.

"Your humble servant, and, though unknown, your friend,

"JOHN CLAYTON."

The writer appears to have returned to England and become Rector of Crofton at Wakefield in Yorkshire. In May, 1688, he prepared for the Royal Society an account of his voyage to Virginia, and the things worthy of observation, which, in 1708, was published at London. Another John Clayton, an eminent botanist and physician, when about twenty years of age, came in 1706 to Virginia, and in 1773 died, aged eighty-seven years. There was also a third John Clayton some years before the Declaration of Independence, who was Attorney-General of the colony.

WILLIAM SELLICK.

William Sellick was in charge of St. Peter's Parish, New Kent, in 1680.

ROBERT CARR.

Robert Carr appears to have been officiating in New Kent for six years from A. D., 1680.

THOMAS VICARS.

Thomas Vicars came to Virginia about 1677, and was connected with the parishes of Gloucester county for twenty years.

JUSTINIAN AYLMER.

Justinian Aylmer, Bishop Meade states, was at Elizabeth City from 1667 to 1690, a period of twenty-three years, yet his name does not appear in 1680 among the Rectors of Virginia.

JOHN SHEPPARD.

John Sheppard appears in Middlesex county as early as 1668, and in 1680 was in charge of Christ's Church parish. Sir Henry Chichely was one of his parishioners.

MINISTERS 1675 TO 1685.

In addition to those we have enumerated, the following ministers were in Virginia between A. D. 1675 and 1688.

Rowland Jones, James City county, A. D. 1674 to 1688.

Paul Williams, Surrey county, A. D. 1680.

Robert Park, Isle of Wight county, A. D. 1680.

William Housden, Isle of Wight county, A. D. 1680.

John Gregory, Nansemond county, A. D. 1680.

John Wood, Nansemond county, A. D. 1680.

John Laurence, Warwick county, A. D. 1680.

William Nern, Norfolk county, A. D. 1680.

James Porter, Norfolk county, A. D. 1680.

Edward Foliott, York county, A. D. 1680.

John Wright, York county, A. D. 1680.

Thomas Taylor, New Kent county, A. D. 1680.

William Williams, New Kent county, A. D. 1680.

Michael Zyperius, Gloucester county, A. D. 1680.

John Gwym, Gloucester county, A. D. 1680.

Charles Davies, Rappahannock county, A. D. 1680.

John Wough, Stafford county, A. D. 1680.

William Butler, Westmoreland county, A. D. 1680.

John Farnefold, Northumberland county, A. D. 1680.

Henry Parker, Accomac county, A. D. 1680.

Benjamin Doggett, Lancaster county, A. D. 1680.

Cope D'Oyley, Elizabeth county, A. D. 1677 to 1687.

CHAPTER IV.

LIFE AND TIMES OF JAMES BLAIR, D.D., FOUNDER AND FIRST RECTOR OF WILLIAM AND MARY COLLEGE.

After the death of Sir William Berkeley, Lord Culpepper, and Lord Howard, of Effingham, in succession, acted as Governors of Virginia, and, though noblemen in name, proved themselves corrupt and avaricious in practice.

During their terms of office there was a large accession of Scotchmen to the population of Virginia. Immediately after the battle of Bothwell's Bridge a number of the hardy insurgents were transported to America, and about the same time another element not quite so desirable. Luttrell, connected with the Government offices of London, writes, in his diary, under date of November 19th, 1692:—"A ship lay in Leith, going for Virginia, on board which the magistrates had ordered fifty lewd women out of the House of Correction, and thirty others who walked the streets after ten at night." In addition to exiled soldiers and bawds, there came, as a foil, men fit to mold a State, men of angular manners, provincial accent, warm hearts, strong minds, and religious principles, whose descendants yet remain a power in the Commonwealth.

In the year 1673 James Blair graduated at the University of Edinburgh, and in time became a Presbyter of the Episcopal Church in Scotland, without Episcopal ordination. Burnet, once Archbishop of Glasgow, who lived in Scotland from A. D. 1643 to 1688, asserts: "No bishop in Scotland, during my stay in that kingdom, ever did so much as desire any of the Presbyters who went over from the Church of Scotland to be re-ordained." Blair, for several years was rector in the parish of Cranston, in Edinburgh county, but relinquished his office, and in 1684 received from the Bishop of Edinburgh, the following certificate:—

"To all concerned. These are to certify and declare that the bearer hereof, Mr. James Blair, presbyter, did officiate in the service of the Holy Ministry, as Rector in the parish of Cranston, in my diocese of Edinburgh for several years preceding the year 1682, with extreme diligence, care and gravity, and did in all the course of his ministry behave himself loyally, peaceably and canonically; and that this is the truth, I certify by these presents, and subscribed with my own hand, the 19th day of August, in the year 1684."

When Blair, in 1685, arrived at Jamestown, he found the social condition the widest contrast to his native land, where the poorest cottager owned a well-thumbed Bible; had reasons for the faith that was in him; and although not clothed "in purple and fine linen," felt that—

"The rank is but the guinea's stamp,
The man's the gowd for a' that."

With no schools in the colony, the planters had grown up in ignorance, and were the tools of a few rich land and slave owners, who, in conjunction with the Governors, enriched themselves by oppressive fees and unjust taxation.

The religion which Blair had learned taught him to think of the common people, and that his calling as a minister of the Gospel would be a failure if their elevation was not secured. His policy, and those of the oligarchy who came to Virginia to grow rich suddenly, did not harmonize, and great heat arose from the contrariety.

When he landed in Virginia he found Thomas Teackle, of lower Accomac, James Sclater, Duel Pead, Jonathan Saunders, Cope D'Oyley, Rowland Jones, and a few other clergymen in the Colony, but they did not possess the "perfervidam vim Scotorum" by which he was characterized.

In 1689 he was appointed the representative of the Bishop of London, with the title of Commissary, but with no power to confirm or ordain.

As a Scotchman, he could not rest until school-teachers were in the land, and he kept up an agitation for a college, both in private and public conferences, until he overcame the objection that education would take planters off from their mechanical employments, and make them grow too knowing to be obedient and submissive. Proceeding to England, on February 8th, 1692–93, the charter for William and Mary College was duly signed, and he and three other clergymen, John Farnefold, Stephen Fouace, who afterwards returned to England, and Stephen Gray, were mentioned therein as among the original trustees. In the preamble to the statutes of the College, published at a very early period, in Latin and English, the condition of Virginia at that time is thus stated:—

"Some few, and very few indeed, of the richer sort sent their children to England to be educated, and there, after many dangers from the seas, and enemies, and unusual distempers occasioned by the change of country and climate, they were often taken off by small-pox and other diseases. It was no wonder if this occasioned a great defect of understanding, and all sorts of literature, and that it was followed with a new generation of men, far short of their forefathers, which, if they had the good fortune, though at a very indifferent rate, to read and write, had no further commerce with the muses, or learned sciences, but spent their life ignobly with the hoe and spade, and other employments of an uncultivated and unpolished country."

Blair, upon his return, was appointed rector of the college, and turned his energies toward the erection of a building at the point afterward known as Williamsburgh. From this time the number of Scotch clergymen increased in the parishes. In 1696 there were ministers with these names: Francis Fordyce, John Alexander, Christopher Anderson, George Robinson, Andrew Monro, John Monro, Blair's brother-in-law, and Andrew Cant, who may have been the son of Andrew Cant, the Presbyterian zealot, who was Professor of Latin, and the parish minister of Aberdeen, handed down to posterity in the well-known lines—

"From Dickson, Henderson and Cant,
Apostles of the Covenant,
Almighty God deliver us."

Andrew, his son, entered the Scotch Episcopal Church, in time became the Bishop of Glasgow, and in 1728 died.

The downright earnestness and strong convictions of Blair roused opposition among the clergy and politicians. Sir Edmund Andros, who was made governor of Virginia, after leaving a memory by no means fragrant in New England, suspended him from the Council, because of his alleged restless "conduct," and the clergy in sympathy with the governor, opposed him because he did not carry on affairs in the high and dry way of the old English rectors.

Nicholas Moreau, a minister of French parentage, on the 12th of April, 1697, writes to the Bishop of Lichfield: "Your clergy in these parts are of very ill example; no discipline nor canons of the Church are observed. The clergy is composed for the most part of Scotchmen, people, indeed, so basely educated, or little acquainted with the executing of their charge and duty, that their lives and conversation are fitter to make heathen than Christians."

Not long before this letter was written, the wife of Commissary Blair was grossly insulted. Philip Ludwell, formerly secretary of the colony, had married the widow of Sir William Berkeley. By invitation Mrs. Blair was accustomed to sit in Lady Berkeley's pew in church. Colonel Daniel Parke, a gay, violent and dissipated man, had become much offended at a sermon which Eburne, the rector, had preached, upon the observance of the seventh commandment, as he had been faithless to his marriage vows. One, day in ill humor, Parke went to church, and finding Mrs. Blair in the pew of Ludwell, who was his father-in-law, he rudely pulled her out.*

A pasquinade printed in A. D. 1704, is very severe upon some of the clergy.

Edward Portlock is lampooned as—

"The cotquean of the age;
A doughty clerk and reverend sage,
Who turns his pulpit to a stage,
And barters reformation;
Rude to his wife, false to his friend,
A clown in conversation."

Jacob Ware, who, from 1690 to 1696 was minister of St. Peter's parish, New Kent, is portrayed as—

"Well warmed and fit for action;
A mongrel parti-colored tool,
Equally mixed of knave and fool,
By nature prone to faction."

Ralph Bowker is stigmatized as—

"A bawling pulpit Hector;
A sot, abandoned to his paunch;
Profane without temptation."

Soloman Whateley, another of the clergy, is—

"A tool no person can describe;
Who sells his conscience for a bribe,
And slights his benefactors."

These lines were probably written by one of the friends of Governor Nicholson, who disliked Blair as much as his predecessor, Sir Edmund Andros. Nicholson was a Gascon in speech and manner. One night, while riding, he met the minister, Stephen Fouace, who came into the colony A.D. 1688, and ordered him not to visit a certain family. When remonstrance was made, the Governor said, excitedly, "When you came hither, you had more rags than bags!" The reply of the clergyman was: "It was no

* Parke had been appointed by Andros Collector and Naval Officer for the Lower James River District. Leaving two daughters in Virginia, he was with the Duke of Marlborough in 1704, and was the Aid who brought to England the news of the victory at Blenheim.

Queen Anne made him Governor of the Leeward Islands; he was very unpopular, and on the 7th of December, 1710, was killed by a mob at Antegoa.

His daughter Lucy married Col. Wm. Byrd, and Fanny became the wife of John Custis, Collector of Customs in Accomac, a descendant of a Rotterdam inn-keeper.

The inscription on his tombstone indicates that he did not have much domestic felicity:—

"Here, under this marble, lies the body of John Custis, Esq., of the city of Williamsburg, Parish of Bruton; formerly of Hungar Parish, on the Eastern Shore of Virginia, and County of Northampton, aged 71 years, and yet he lived but 7 years, which was the space of time he kept a bachelor's home, at Arlington, on the Eastern Shore of Virginia."

His son, John Parke Custis, married Martha Dandridge. When a widow, Martha Custis, she was married to the great George Washington.

harm to have been poor." The Governor then rode up and pulled his hat from his head, and asked how he had the impudence to ride in his presence with covered head.

The dispute between Governor Nicholson and Blair divided the colony into parties. Nicholson wrote to the Home Government concerning the Blair faction; "If they had the power of using the Scotch way of using the thummikins, or the French way of the rack, or the Barbary way of impaling or twisting a cord about peoples' heads, to make them confess, they would scarcely find any to swear up to what they would have them." In another letter he writes of Blair: "He might have had a sort of spiritual militia, but into whom, no doubt, he would have endeavored to have infused some worldly principles, as that they might have enjoyed a comfortable terrestrial subsistence before they had endeavored to have secured themselves a celestial habitation."

Blair, in 1705, was relieved of Nicholson's abuse, by his recall and the appointment of Edward Nott as deputy of Earl of Orkney, Governor.

By the year 1700 a number of French clergymen had been licensed by the Bishop of London to preach in Virginia, and we find the names of Moreau, Boisseau, Burtell and Lewis Latané, the ancestor of the esteemed Presbyter of the Reformed Episcopal Church who bears the same name.

The inhabitants divided into parties upon questions of public policy, leading to angry discussion and social alienation, many of the clergy preaching for the love of money, rather than constrained by the love of Christ, it is not surprising that plain people began to attach themselves to the Society of Friends, whose ministers accepted no compensation, and that not a few in high places were influenced by their earnest declarations concerning the love of Christ for sinners.

Before Blair left the University of Edinburgh, Richard Bennett, who had been Governor of Virginia, a man of wealth and influence, had sympathized with the Friends in his neighborhood in Nansemond county, one of whom was John Copeland, whose ear had been cut off in Boston in 1658, as a disturber of the peace.

In A. D. 1698 there appeared another disciple of Fox in Virginia, named Thomas Story, a brother of the Dean of Lismore, of the Church of England and Ireland, fully the equal of Blair in culture, scholarship, and logical acumen. Toward the close of 1698, O.S., he held the first Friends' meeting at Yorktown. Two days later he was at the house of Thomas Cary, in Warwick, who, with his wife, had lately become Friends, and while visiting there, Miles Cary and his wife "were made partakers of the heavenly visitation."

Crossing the James river into Nansemond, he stopped at the house of the aged Copeland, whose single ear attested what he had lost and suffered for the faith, in Boston, forty years before. On the 10th of the Second month, 1699, he visited the Chickahominy village, of eleven wigwams, on Pamunkey neck, and then went one mile, to the house of a son of the distinguished William Clayborne, for many years secretary of the Colony. Two weeks later he preaches at the house of a Baptist minister in Yorktown, and from thence travels to Pocoson, where he found a large congregation, and was entertained by Thomas Nichols and wife, the latter, he says, in his journal, "though a mulatto by extraction, yet not too tawny for the divine light of the Lord Jesus Christ." At Kecoughtan, now Hampton, he tarried with George Walker, whose wife was the daughter of the once noted Quaker preacher, George Keith.

A second visitation was made by Story, in A.D. 1705. On the 26th of the Fourth month he was at Williamsburgh, conversing with Governor Nicholson upon the reasonableness of "all people that are of opinion that they ought to pay their preachers paying their own, and not exacting pay from others who do not employ nor hear them." Two days afterward he called at the house of Miles Cary, Secretary of Warwick county. On the 5th of the Seventh month his traveling companion, Joseph Glaister, had a discussion with Andrew Monro, a Scotch clergyman, at the mansion of Colonel Bridges, at the south side of the James river. The weather being hot, Monro, who was an elderly man, became so faint and weary as scarcely to be heard; at length he called for a pipe of tobacco and a tankard of ale, and soon, on his part, the discussion "ended in drink and smoke."

Five days afterwards James Burtell, the French clergyman, came to the house of Thomas Jordan, a county judge, to hold a public discussion with Story, as to the baptism intended in the words of Jesus Christ: "Go ye, therefore, and teach all nations, baptizing them in the name of the Father, and of the Son, and of the Holy Ghost."

Burtell affirmed that water baptism only was commanded. Story argued that the baptism of the Holy Ghost was intended. "I grant," said the latter, "the apostles could not baptize with the Holy Ghost at their own pleasure, when and whom and where they would, in their own wills, as your ministers can and do administer what they call, and have taught you, Christ's baptism; but that the apostles could not instrumentally baptize with the Holy Ghost, I deny." * * * * At the same time he referred to the text, "Go ye into all the world and preach the Gospel to every creature. He that believeth and is baptized shall be saved; but he that believeth not shall be damned." And that this was not water baptism plainly appeareth, for Jesus said: "John truly baptizeth with water, but ye shall be baptized with the Holy Ghost not many days hence."

Story, also, declared that the baptism here spoken of was contra-distinguished from John's baptism, and could only be administered by the power of the Holy Ghost, co-working in them, with them, and by them.

These discussions caused the people to "search the Scriptures," and those clergymen who did not lay stress upon the power of the Holy Spirit had but few hearers.

Blair, amid all of the distractions within his own branch of the Church, and the controversies caused by the presence of Friends' preachers, was studious and faithful in his sermons. At a Convention of the Episcopal clergy, in A.D. 1719, held at Williamsburgh, the question was considered, whether the Commissary had ever been Episcopally ordained? A majority voted that they had no evidence of the fact. The men who placed themselves on record upon this point, were Pownal, Seagood, Emanuel Jones, Lewis Latané, Bartholomew Yates, John Skaife, Hugh Jones, John Worden, John Bagge, James Falconer, Alexander Scott, and Ralph Bowker.

Yates was one of the most devoted clergymen in the Colony. Ordained at Fulham, by the Bishop of London, in A.D. 1710, he arrived in Virginia, and became the minister of Christ Church parish, in Middlesex county. He was chosen Professor of Divinity in William and Mary College, but still continued rector of his old parish, until July 26th, 1734, the day of his death. Not far from the Rappahannock river, in a deserted churchyard, is now seen the stone over his remains, erected by his parishioners, and the inscription thereon states that he was a tender husband, indulgent father, gentle master, and that "he explained his doctrine by his practice, and taught and led the way to heaven."

Lewis Latané, another respected minister, came to the Colony about the year 1700, and for twenty-three years preached in South Farnham parish, Essex county.

Emanuel Jones, of Petworth, Gloucester county, arrived the same time as Latané, and was a tutor of the college.

Skaife, who had been a curate in Cambridgeshire and Bedfordshire, came to Virginia, in 1708, and for many years had the charge of the parish of Stratton Major, in King and Queen county, and was one of the trustees of the college.

Bagge had been a curate in the diocese of Lismore, and in 1709 came to the Colony.

Hugh Jones arrived in Maryland 1698; about 1703 was elected Professor of Mathematics in William and Mary College. In 1724 there was published at London a duodecimo of one hundred and fifty pages, with the title, "The Present State of Virginia, and Short View of Maryland and North Carolina. By Rev. Hugh Jones, A.M., Chaplain to the Honorable Assembly, and late Minister at Jamestown, Virginia."

The book contains the following description of the mode of worship during the term of Commissary Blair.

"In several respects the clergy are obliged to omit or alter parts of the Liturgy, and deviate from the strict discipline, to avoid giving offense, or else to prevent absurdities and inconsistencies. Thus surplices disused there for a long time in most churches, by bad examples, carelessness and indulgence, are now beginning to be brought into fashion, not without difficulty; and in some parishes where the people have been used to receive the communion in their seats, a custom introduced for opportunity for such as were inclined to presbytery to receive the sacrament sitting, it is not so easy a matter to bring them to the Lord's table, decently, on their knees."

At the time of this publication, the college at Williamsburgh is described as "without a chapel, without a scholarship, without a statute." On the 28th of June, 1732, the College chapel was opened by President Blair, preaching a sermon from Proverbs xxii, 6. "Train up a child in the way he should go, and when he is old he will not depart from it." A year later the foundation for the President's house was laid, the President and each of the faculty laying one of the first five bricks.

About the year 1700 the African population began to increase. Governor Nicholson writes in July of that year, that negroes were bringing "from twenty-eight to thirty guineas a head," and adds, "I believe two thousand would sell." In 1712 the Governor of Virginia announced that one-half of the population capable of bearing arms was composed of negroes and indentured servants.

In the Legislature of 1722–23 a law relative to suffrage was passed, which caused some discussion.

For almost a half century after the settlement at Jamestown universal suffrage prevailed, but in 1653 it was limited to "all housekeepers, freeholders, leaseholders or tenants," but two years after universal suffrage was restored, with the proviso that the votes were to be given by subscription instead of *viva voce*, and the Act was prefaced with a preamble stating that the Assembly conceived "it something hard and unagreeable to reason that any persons shall pay taxes and have no votes in election."

After the restoration of monarchy in England, and the return of Sir William Berkeley to the governorship, suffrage was again restricted to freeholders and householders. The preamble of the Act of 1670 is in these words:—

"Whereas the usual way of choosing burgesses by the votes of all persons, who, having served their time, are freemen; who having little interest in this country, do oftener make tumults at the election, than by making choice of fit persons, and whereas the laws of England grant a voice in such elections only to such as by their estates, real or personal, have interest enough to tie them to the endeavor of the public good;" then followed the restrictive clause, already alluded to.

In a few years the republican feeling was strengthened by Bacon and others, and in 1676 the restrictive clause was revoked, and universal suffrage again became the law of the land.

Eight years pass, and in 1684 it is again enacted that none but freeholders should exercise the right of suffrage. It was not until more than a hundred years after the meeting of the first legislative assembly that any effort was made to prevent the voting of Indians or free negroes. The Assembly of 1722–23, however, enacted that "no free negro, mulatto, or Indian whatsoever shall have any vote at the election of burgesses or any other election whatsoever." As required, the statutes passed by this Assembly were sent over to England for approval by the Commissioners of Trade and Plantations, and they were referred to their attorney, Richard West, afterward Lord Chancellor of Ireland, for examination. He reported adversely to the restrictive suffrage, using this language, "I cannot see why one free-man should be used worse than another, merely upon account of his complexion."

But, notwithstanding the opinion of the jurist, the Commissioners allowed the law to exist. When George Mason drew the first Declaration of Rights in America, which was adopted by the Virginia Convention in June, 1776, as part of their first Constitution, he reincorporated the idea set forth in the Suffrage Law of 1656, that it was "something hard and unagreeable to reason that any persons shall pay taxes and have no votes in election."

The sixth Article of the Declaration of Rights was in these words:—

"That elections of members to serve as representatives of the people in the Legislature ought to be free, and that all men having sufficient evidence of permanent, common interest with, and attachment to, the community, have the right of suffrage, and cannot be taxed or deprived of their property for public uses without their own consent, or that of their representative so elected, nor bound by any law to which they have not in like manner assented, for the common good."

Amid all the distractions of an active life, Commissary Blair found time to prepare one hundred and seventeen discourses on the sermon on the Mount, which were first published in London, in five octavo volumes. Dr. Doddridge, the Scripture expositor, pronounced it the best commentary on the fifth, sixth and seventh chapters of Matthew extant, and adds:—

"He appears to have been a person of the utmost candor, and has solicitously avoided all unkind and contemptuous reflections on his brethren. He has an excellent way of bringing down criticism to common capacities, and has discovered a vast knowledge of Scripture, in the application of them." A second edition of the work appeared in 1740, in four volumes, with a preface by Bishop Waterland.

George Whitfield, in his Diary, under date of 15th of December, 1740, writes:

"Paid my respects to Mr. Blair, Commissary of Virginia. His discourse was savory, such as tended to the use of edifying. He received me with joy, asked me to preach, and wished my stay were longer."

In 1743, after a ministry in Virginia of more than fifty years, he died, having proved himself an "*emeritus miles*," by "enduring hardness as a good soldier of Christ."

His son John, lived to see the independence of the United States of America, and to be one of the first judges of the Supreme Court, appointed by President Washington.

CHAPTER VI.

LIFE AND TIMES OF JONATHAN BOUCHER, THE TORY CLERGYMAN, A.D. 1759–1775.

Jonathan Boucher was one of the best representatives of the colonial clergy, from the period succeeding the defeat of Braddock until the colonies declared themselves free and independent States.

He was born on the 12th of March, 1738, at Blencogo, in Cumberland county, England. While completing his education in mathematics, under the direction of a Rev. Mr. Ritson, who lived at Workington, near the mouth of the Derwent, he received an appointment as private tutor in the family of Captain Dixon, who lived on the Rappahannock river.

In July, 1759, he reached his destination at Port Royal. In his autobiography he writes: "Being hospitable, as well as wealthy, Captain Dixon's house was much resorted to, but chiefly by toddy-drinking company. Port Royal was chiefly inhabited by factors from Scotland, and their dependents, and the circumjacent country by planters in general, in middling circumstances. There was not a literary man, for aught I could find, nearer than in the country I had just left, nor were literary attainments, beyond merely reading or writing, at all in vogue."

In A.D. 1761, he was unexpectedly asked to enter the ministry. A Rev. Mr. Giberne, who lived on the north side of the Rappahannock, opposite Port Royal, about to marry a rich widow in Richmond county, resigned his parish, and the vestry asked him to fill the vacancy. He went to London, was ordained by Bishop Osbaldiston, and in July, 1762, became the rector of the parish in King George county, and preached at Leeds. In less than six months he was called to a parish near Port Royal, in Caroline county, made vacant by the death of the Rev. Thomas Dawson, Commissary of Virginia, which he accepted.

In the spring of 1763 he moved to this new field of labor, and remained seven years. Here he established a boarding school in his own house, and at one time had thirty pupils. Among his pupils was John Parke Custis, the step-son of General Washington. "This," says he, "laid the foundation of a very particular intimacy and friendship, which lasted till we finally separated, never to unite again, on our taking different sides in the late troubles.

"Mr. Washington was the second of five sons, of parents distinguished neither for their rank, nor fortune. Lawrence, their eldest son, became a soldier, and went on the expedition to Carthagena, where, getting into some scrape with a brother officer, it was said he did not acquit himself quite so well as he ought, and so sold out.

"George, who, like most people thereabouts at that time, had no other education than reading, writing and accounts, which he was taught by a convict servant, whom his father bought for a schoolmaster, first set out in the world as Surveyor of Orange County, an appointment of about half the value of a Virginia Rectory, perhaps £100 a year.

"When the French made encroachments on the Western Frontier, in 1754, this Washington was sent out to examine, on, the spot, how far what was alleged was true, and to remonstrate on the occasion. He published his journal, which in Virginia, at least, drew on him some ridicule. * * * * * * At Braddock's defeat, and every subsequent occasion throughout the war, he acquitted himself much in the same manner as, in my judgment, he has since done, decently, but never greatly. I did know Mr. Washington well. * * * * * * * He is shy, silent, stern, slow and cautious. * * * * In his moral character, he is regular, temperate, strictly just and honest, and, as I always thought, religious, having heretofore been pretty constant, and even exemplary in his attendance on public worship in the Church of England. But he seems to have nothing generous or affectionate in his nature. Just before the close of the last war he married the widow Custis, and thus came into the possession of her large jointure. He never had any children, and lived very much like a gentleman, at Mount Vernon, in Fairfax County, where the most distinguished part of his character was, that he was an admirable farmer."

This estimate of Washington, from a Tory, can now be perused with complacency, since the world has long ago declared—

> "He was a man; take him for all in all,
> I shall not look upon his like again."

The French charged that Washington, under excitement, fired upon Jumonville, the French commander, while he was bearing a flag of truce. De Villiers, in his report of Washington's surrender at Fort Necessity, wrote:—

"We made the English consent to sign that they had *assassinated my brother*." In the articles of agreement it is so written. In 1756, these facts were brought to light by William Livingston, of New Jersey, and no doubt caused some criticism and ridicule of Washington.

Boucher, in one of his sermons, gives a picture of the bald and desolate appearance of the parish churches at the period of the Revolution. He remarks: "Our churches in general are ordinary and mean buildings, composed of wood, without spires or towers, or steeples or bells, and placed, for the most part, like those of our remotest ancestors in Great Britain, in retired and solitary spots, and contiguous to springs or wells. Within them, there is rarely even an attempt to introduce any ornaments; it is almost as uncommon to find a church that has any communion plate, as it is in England to find one that has not; in both Virginia and Maryland, there are not six organs; the Psalmody is everywhere ordinary and mean, and in not a few places there is none."

Unlike Blair, he had no sympathy, with Whitfield and his followers. Davies, more than his equal in eloquence, scholarship and spirituality, afterward President of Princeton, he looked down upon as a common dissenter. He used every means to prevent the growth of nonconformity, and in one of his sermons regrets its increase, and stated that thirty years ago there was not a dissenting congregation in Virginia, while then there were eleven ministers, and each with from two to four congregations.

In his autobiography he remarks, "I attributed much of my success in this (keeping down nonconformists), to my avoiding all disputation with their ministers, whom I spoke of as beneath such condescension, on the score of their ignorance and their impudence. And when one of them publicly challenged me to a public debate, I declined it, but at the same time set up one Daniel Barksdale, a carpenter in my parish, who had a good front, and a voluble tongue, and whom, therefore, I easily qualified to defeat his opponent, as he effectually did. And I am still persuaded that this method, of treating the preachers with well-judged ridicule and contempt, and their followers with gentleness, persuasion, and attention, is a good one."

Upon the subject of African slavery, he held the views of Henry, Jefferson and Washington. Destitute of moral cowardice, in 1763 he preached a sermon, in which he remarked—

"Were an impartial and comprehensive observer of the state of society in these Middle Colonies asked whence it happened that Virginia and Maryland, which were the first planted, and are superior to many colonies, and inferior to none in point of every natural advantage, are still so exceedingly behind most of the other British American Provinces, in all those improvements which bring credit and consequence to a country? he would answer: They are so, because they are cultivated by slaves. I believe it is capable of demonstration, that except the money interest which every man has in the property of his slaves, it would be for every man's interest that there were no slaves, and for this plain reason, because the free labor of a free man, who is regularly hired and paid for the work which he does, is in the end cheaper than the extorted eye-service of a slave. Some loss and inconvenience would no doubt arise from the general abolition of slavery in the Colonies, but were it done gradually, with judgment and good temper, I have never yet seen it satisfactorily proved that such injury would be either great or lasting."

During Boucher's residence in Caroline County, he manifested an interest for the slaves, and on the 31st of March, 1766, Easter Monday, baptized three hundred and thirteen negro adults, and preached to upwards of a thousand. He, moreover, employed two or three intelligent blacks to teach the children on Sunday afternoons. In time, twenty or thirty were able to use the Prayer-book at the Sunday services, and thirteen became communicants.

Calm and fearless in manner, logical and intellectual in his discourses, he succeeded in obtaining the entire respect of the planters among whom he resided. In one of his sermons he states that "he had lived among them more than seven years, as minister, in such harmony as to have had no disagreement with any man, even for a day." While in Virginia, he was intimate with the Rev. James Maury or Marye, a clergyman, of French parentage, born at sea, trained in England, educated in America, and settled in Albemarle county. At Maury's request, he wrote a poem, which was well received, on the dispute between the Clergy and the Assembly of Virginia, relative to the injustice of the act allowing two pence a pound to be paid instead of the 16,000 pounds of tobacco in kind, due as salary of a parish minister.

In 1770, he left Virginia, to become Rector of the church at Annapolis, the capital of Maryland, and took with him his pupil, John Parke Custis, the step-son of Washington.

The State House now used by the legislature of Maryland had not then been erected, and the church edifice was in a dilapidated condition, while the town boasted a handsome theater, in which Hallam and others played, built on land owned by the church. To stimulate his parishioners to the erection of a new church, he published, soon after he became the Rector of St. Anne's, in the Maryland *Gazette*, a poetical epistle, addressed:—

"*To the very worthy and respectable inhabitants of Annapolis, the humble petition of the old Church sheweth:—*"

A portion of this effusion is as follows:

"That late in Century the last,
By private bounty, here were placed
My sacred walls, and tho' in truth
Their stile and manner be uncouth,
Yet whilst no structure met mine eye
That even with myself could vie,
A goodly edifice, I seemed,
And pride of all St. Anne's was deemed.
How changed the times! for now all round
Unnumbered stately piles abound,
All better built and looking down
On one quite antiquated grown:
Left unrepaired, to time a prey,
I feel my vitals fast decay;
And often have I heard it said
That some good people are afraid
Lest I should tumble, on their head,
Of which, indeed, this seems a proof,
They seldom come beneath my roof.
* * * * * *
Here in Annapolis, alone,
God has the meanest house in town.
The premises considered, I,
With humble confidence, rely,
That, Phœnix like, I soon shall rise,
From my own ashes, to the skies;
Your mite, at least, that you will pay,
And your petitioner shall pray."

While residing in Annapolis he determined to know something besides "Jesus Christ and Him crucified." He became much absorbed in the social, literary and political pursuits of the community. He wrote some verses on an actress, and a prologue for the theater, and was made first President of the Hominy Club, a society formed to promote innocent mirth. He was recognized as Governor Eden's right hand man and most intimate friend. He says: "I was, in fact, the most efficient person in the administration of Government. The management of the Assembly was left very much to me, and hardly a Bill was brought in which I did not either draw, or at least revise." The Governor's speeches, messages and other important papers were also from his pen. In the defense of what he supposed were the rights of the Maryland clergy, he had a sharp controversy with two lawyers, William Paca and Samuel Chase, both of whom, in 1776, were in the Continental Congress, and signers of the Declaration. Paca, smarting under some remark, was disposed to fight a duel with the rector of St. Anne's, but was quieted by the gentleman whom he consulted as his second.

Governor Eden, who valued his talents and friendship, in 1772 offered him the lower church of Queen Anne's Parish, Prince George county, Md., which he accepted. About this time he was married to a Miss Addison, a native of this county, niece of the Rev. Henry Addison, educated at Queen's College, Oxford, daughter of Thomas Addison, and grandchild of John Addison, Surveyor-General of the Province of Maryland.

His controversy with the lawyers, Paca and Chase, gave him a reputation among the Episcopal clergy of New York and New England, and King's College, now Columbia, in New York city, conferred upon him the degree of Master of Arts. The Rev. Dr. Cooper, President of King's College, visited him, and in company they proceeded to the residence of Rev. Dr. Smith, Provost of the College of Philadelphia, to concert measures to support the Mother Country in the pending controversies. "It is too well known," he says, "how little the clergy of Philadelphia regarded this agreement."

The ancestral residence of his wife's family was at Oxon Hall, nearly opposite Alexandria. In his reminiscences he writes:

"I happened to be going across the Potomac with my wife and some other of our friends, exactly at the time that General Washington was crossing it on his way to the northward, whither he was going to take command of the Continental army. There had been a great meeting of people, and great doings in Alexandria on the occasion; and everybody seemed to be on fire, either with rum or patriotism, or both. Some patriots in our boat huzzaed, and gave three cheers to the General as he passed us, while Mr. Addison and myself contented ourselves with pulling off our hats. Then General (then only Colonel) Washington beckoned us to stop, as we did, just to shake us by the hand, he said.

"His behavior to me was now, as it had always been, polite and respectful, and I shall forever remember what passed in the few disturbed moments of conversation we then had. From his going on his present errand, I foresaw and apprised him of much that has since happened; in particular, that there would certainly then be a civil war, and that the Americans would soon declare for independency. With more earnestness than was usual with his great reserve, he scouted my apprehensions, adding, and I believe with perfect sincerity, that if ever I heard of his joining in such measures, I had his leave to set him down for everything wicked. * * * * This was the last time I ever saw this gentleman, who, contrary to all reasonable expectation, has since so distinguished himself, that he will probably be handed down to posterity as one of the first characters of the age."

From this period, party feeling deepened in Maryland, and Boucher thought it prudent to leave his residence in the lower parish of Prince George county, and he removed to the "Lodge," the home of Rev. Henry Addison, his wife's uncle, in the upper part of the county. During his absence, services were held by his curate, a Republican, a brother of Robert Hanson Harrison, one of Washington's aids. He became increasingly unpopular, and whenever he preached there was more or less disapprobation. "For more than six months" he writes, "I preached, when I did preach, with a pair of loaded pistols lying on the cushion, having given notice that if any man or body of men could possibly be so lost to all sense of decency and propriety as to drag me out of my own pulpit, I should think myself justified before God and man in repelling violence."

In 1775 the Republican authorities set apart Thursday, the 11th day of May, for prayer and fasting, and Mr. Boucher announced that he would preach in his own pulpit. The text he had chosen was from Nehemiah vi, 10, 11: "Afterward I came unto the house of Shemaiah, the son of Delaiah, the son of Mehetabeel, who was shut up; and he said, let us meet together in the house of God, within the temple, and let us shut the doors of the temple, for they will come to slay thee; yea, in the night will they come to slay thee. And I said, should such a man as I flee? and who is there that, being as I am, would go into the temple to save his life? I will not go in."

Fifteen minutes before the time of service he arrived at the church, but found the Republican curate, Harrison, already in the desk, and a crowd of armed men around the church. A Mr. Osborne Sprigg, who was the leader, told him that they did not wish him to preach. He replied that they would have, then, to take away his life; and with sermon in one hand, and a loaded pistol in the other, moved toward the pulpit, but was instantly surrounded by excited men. Seizing Sprigg by the collar of his coat, and with cocked pistol, he told him he would blow his brains out if any of the crowd should dare attack him. The crowd, while not injuring him, forced him out of the church, and escorted him to his residence, a fifer playing the tune of the "Rogue's March." Fearless and persevering, he appeared at the church next Sunday, and, amid much confusion, preached the sermon he had prepared for "Fast-day."

From this time his feelings were embittered against the Republicans, and on the 16th of August, 1775, he wrote, under excitement, a long letter to Washington, which he concludes in these words:—

"I have, at least, the merit of consistency; and neither in any private or public conversation, in anything I have written, nor in anything that I have delivered from the pulpit, have I ever asserted any other opinions or doctrines than you have repeatedly heard me assert, both in my own house and yours. You cannot say that I deserved to be run down, villified, and injured in the manner which you know has fallen to my lot, merely because I cannot bring myself to think, on some political points, just as you and your party would have me think. And yet you have borne to look on, at least as an unconcerned spectator, if not an abetter, whilst, like the poor frogs in the fable, I have in a manner been pelted to death. I do not ask if such conduct in you was friendly; was it either, just, manly, or generous? It was not; no, it was acting with all the base malignity of a virulent Whig. As such, Sir, I resent it; and oppressed and overborne as I may seem to be, by popular obloquy, I will not be so wanting in justice to myself as not to tell you, as I now do, with honest boldness, that I despise the man who, for any motives, could be induced to act so mean a part. You are no longer worthy of my friendship; a man of honor can no longer, without dishonor, be connected with you. With your cause, I renounce you."

In this frame of mind, he became odious to the friends of Congress, and in a month was a refugee.

On the 10th of September, with his wife and her uncle, the Rev. Henry Addison, and his son, he went on board a small schooner, the *Nell Gwynn*, and, sailing down the Potomac, entered the Chesapeake, and was taken aboard a vessel, which, on the 20th of October, reached Dover, in England. For nineteen years he was Vicar of Epsom, and devoted much time to philological studies. He died, A.D. 1804, at the age of sixty-six years. His engraved portrait shows a firm, benevolent, round-faced man, with expansive forehead.

In 1797 he published "A View of the Causes and Consequences of the American Revolution," which he gracefully dedicated as a kind of peace offering to his old friend, who had been the first president of the United States of America. Washington, in reply to the compliment, in a letter from Mount Vernon, dated 15th of August, 1798, wrote, "For the honor of its dedication and for the friendly and favorable sentiments therein expressed, I pray you to accept my acknowledgment and thanks. Not having read the book, it follows, of course, that I can express no opinion with respect to its political contents, but I can venture to assert beforehand, and with confidence, that there is no man in either country more zealously devoted to peace and a good understanding between the nations than I am: no one who is more disposed to bury in oblivion all animosities which have subsisted between them and the individuals of each."

He was married three times. His first wife, Miss Addison, noted for her beauty, had no children, neither had the second. By his third wife he had several children, one of whom was the Rev. Barton Boucher, of Wiltshire. It was not until 1871 his last child, a daughter, died. One of his grandsons, bearing his name, is a valued contributor to the London *Notes and Queries*, and to him we are indebted for extracts from his grandfather's journals.

In concluding this article, a brief reference will not be out of place, to Rev. Walter Dulaney Addison, who became Rector of the parish from which his uncle had been ejected a few months before the Declaration of Independence. He was the son of Thomas Addison, whose wife was Rebecca Dulaney, of Annapolis; and also the nephew of the wife of Jonathan Boucher. In 1788, while on a visit to his uncle, by marriage, in England, Mr. Boucher requested him to make a catalogue of his library. In doing this, he fell from a ladder while examining some books on a high shelf, and was much injured. While confined to his room he became very serious, and determined to enter the ministry. Returning to this country he married a Miss Hesselius, of Annapolis, and then went to reside with his mother at Oxon Hall, on the Potomac. For several years he occupied the same pulpits which Jonathan Boucher had preached from in Prince George county, and formed a wide contrast to his relative in his views of religion. With what was considered Puritanic strictness, he frowned upon duelling, horse racing, card playing, and theater-going. While attached to the liturgy of his Church, he maintained friendly relations with those whom he recognized as ministers of other branches of the Church. For many years he was deprived of sight. God took him, in 1848, ripe in age, and fit for heaven. His friends deposited his remains in the burial place of his ancestors, at Oxon Hall.

FINIS.

A PLAINT

OF SAMUEL PURCHAS, RECTOR OF ST. MARTIN'S, LUDGATE, LONDON, A.D., 1625.

"My prayers shall be to the Almighty for Virginia's prosperity, whose dwarfish growth after so many years' convulsions by dissensions, Tantalean starvings amidst rich magazines and fertilities, subversion here and self eversion there (perverseness I mention not), rather than conversion of savages, after so many learned and holy men sent there; poverty, sickness, death in such a soil and healthful climate—what shall I say?

"I can deplore, I do not much admire, that we have had so much in Virginia, yet so little; the promises as probable as large, and yet the premises yielding, in the conclusion, this Virginian sterility and meagerness, rather than the multiplied issue and thrift of a worthy nation, and mother of a family answering to her great inheritance. But what do I in plaints, when some, perhaps, will complain of my complainings?"

www.ingramcontent.com/pod-product-compliance
Lightning Source LLC
LaVergne TN
LVHW021422110826
845150LV00007B/2043

* 9 7 8 1 4 2 5 5 0 8 7 9 1 *